PRAISE FOR CAROLYN B. JOSEPHS

Carolyn's holistic approach to SEO is bar none! She takes the time to get to know every aspect of your business. Her attention to detail and her customer service adds value that allows her to formulate a more effective plan than most of her competition. Carolyn's experience, dedication, and ability to get results for her clients makes her the go to person for SEO. If you are looking for someone who delivers the whole SEO experience for your company, I highly recommend Carolyn! Carolyn gets RESULTS!!!

LISA CHALKER, MULTIPRENEUR – FINANCIAL EDUCATOR

Carolyn combines creativity with business acumen and therefore is able to effectively help her clients with their email marketing and social media needs. She's incredibly responsive and leaves no stone unturned in her efforts to provide the highest quality work. Her focus is on small to mid-sized businesses and that means she understands "our" needs and wants and she can scale with us as we grow. I recommend that you connect with Carolyn and see what a professional email marketer can do for your business.

ADRIAN MILLER, ADRIAN MILLER SALES TRAINING

Carolyn has worked with me on my marketing materials for my collection these past 2 seasons. This season she saved us by redoing many images for us in a VERY short period of time. Carolyn will go the extra mile. My staff and I couldn't be happier with the work that she did!

AIMEE GRUBEL, TEXTILE RESOURCE, GM,
FASHION DESIGN, PRODUCTION
MANAGEMENT

I met Carolyn Josephs through a networking group and we started sharing our joint experience in building websites and driving traffic to websites. I was particularly impressed with her broad knowledge of SEO and her significant experience in working with owners of websites to drive traffic to their websites. And equally important is that I really enjoyed working with her. I would highly recommend her to anyone looking to drive traffic to their website.

RICHARD STRAUTMAN, EXECUTIVE COACH,
EXIT PLANNER, FACILITATOR WITH COMPEL
CEO'S, CEO MENTORING, LEADERSHIP, AND
BUSINESS GROWTH CONSULTING

36

Ways To Improve Your

SEARCH ENGINE OPTIMIZATION

An Interactive Workbook
to Drive RESULTS!

CAROLYN B. JOSEPHS

Published by Red Penguin Books

Bellerose Village, New York

Library of Congress Control Number: 2022916896

ISBN

Print 978-1-63777-310-9

Digital 978-1-63777-311-6

Google Business Page is a registered trademark of Google LLC and Alphabet, Inc., as well as its affiliates in the United States and around the world.

This book is dedicated to my husband, Greg, without whose support this book would not be possible and in memory of Kay & Lenny Josephs.

RIP Mom & Dad. I will never forget you!

CONTENTS

CHAPTER 1
WHAT IS SEARCH ENGINE OPTIMIZATION (SEO)?

Search engine optimization (SEO) is the process of improving the visibility of a website or webpage on a search engine results page (SERP) to make a company's website more discoverable (i.e., on the first page), thereby driving traffic and sales. The work can be very tedious, involves technical and business decisions, and does not guarantee results. However, it provides lasting benefits.

SEO often involves the concerted effort of multiple departments within an organization, including the design, marketing, and content production teams. Much of the success of SEO depends on the *ranking algorithms* of various search engines, which change with time. Nevertheless, a rule of thumb is that websites and webpages with higher-quality content, more external referral links, and more user engagement will rank higher on an SERP.

The SEO process includes six general phases:

1. **Research**, including business research, competitor analysis, current state assessment, and keyword searching.
2. **Planning and Strategy**, including decisions on how to handle content, build links to the website, manage social media presence, and technical implementation strategies.

3. **Implementation**, where optimization decisions on a site's web pages and the website as a whole are executed.
4. **Monitoring**, where the activity of web spiders, traffic, search engine rankings, and other metrics are observed for producing reports on which assessment will be performed.
5. **Assessment**, involves checking the summarized effects of the strategy (and its implementation) against the SEO process's stated targets.
6. **Maintenance**, where both minor or major problems with the website's operation are handled as they arise (i.e., new content that needs optimization according to the strategy).

The SEO process targets mostly organic links and search engine result placement.

Throughout this workbook tips become actions steps as the reader is guided into improving their own site's SEO.

CHAPTER 2
TYPES OF SEO

When optimizing a website for search engines, you must consider hundreds of rules to satisfy the various search engine ranking factors and simultaneously keep your users happy. This is not an easy task. To make it easier to handle, the SEO industry came up with different types of SEO. Each type is responsible for several SEO rules.

What is important to understand is that these subsets of SEO are not different processes. It's just a way of breaking down a complicated process into several smaller processes that are easier to manage.

The most important are On-Page, Off-Page, and Technical SEO, as shown in the diagram above. There are, however, other types of SEO that should be recognized.

WHAT YOU NEED TO KNOW ABOUT ON-PAGE SEO

On-Page SEO is the component of SEO that focuses on optimizing elements on your website, like page speed and keyword density, versus factors outside your website, like backlinks.

On-Page SEO is important because it gives Google, as well as the other search engines, all the information about your website, content, and how you bring value to your audience and customers. This technique helps you optimize your site for people and search engines. There are over 1.7 billion websites so just creating and launching a website is not enough, as your target audience won't find your business. Google and other search engines will not rank you, therefore, you need to optimize it to increase your search engine rankings and attract new traffic. As the search engine algorithm becomes more sophisticated, we strongly recommend that you focus on writing for humans and not algorithms.

To rank your content today, you need to optimize your content for user experience, bounce rate, dwell time, search intent, page loading speed and click-through rate as well as keywords. *Keep in mind that you want to make sure you are offering valuable content to your audience. While the algorithm is important, don't focus on it. It is always best to use the current best practices so it is critical to stay on top of them.*

On the next page or a separate piece of paper, go through all your web pages and make sure all of your content (both text & images) is SEO-optimized.

WAYS I AM IMPROVING MY ON-PAGE SEO

1. _____

2. _____

3. _____

4. _____

5. _____

6. _____

7. _____

8. _____

9. _____

10. _____

11. _____

12. _____

13. _____

14. _____

15. _____

16. _____

17. _____

18. _____

19. _____

20. _____

21. _____

22. _____

23. _____

24. _____

25. _____

26. _____

27. _____

28. _____

29. _____

30. _____

31. _____

32. _____

33. _____

34. _____

35. _____

36. _____

37. _____

38. _____

39. _____

40. _____

41. _____

42. _____

43. _____

44. _____

45. _____

46. _____

47. _____

48. _____

49. _____

50. _____

51. _____

52. _____

53. _____

54. _____

55. _____

56. _____

57. _____

58. _____

59. _____

60._____

CHAPTER 3
DON'T GET OFF TRACK
WITH OFF-PAGE SEO

While the previous chapter concentrated more on On-Page SEO, Off-Page SEO has to do with techniques you can use to promote your website on the Internet. Popular websites are more likely to rank higher on Google than less popular websites.

Off-Page SEO helps you to bring in visitors and potential customers. By writing quality content you can rank in search engines, but by getting a few great, relevant sites to link to that content, you're increasing the chance that you'll end up a couple of spots higher. Building your brand and creating trust doesn't just happen on your site, it happens mostly off-site. Reviews, for example, can make or break your company. You need them, but they most often appear on external sites. These are all factors that contribute to your rankings. It's not only important for you to rank high for your search term, but also to create trust and a sense of authority. You must appear to be the best search result.

A lot of Off-Page SEO comes down to link-building. Links are the glue that keeps the web together. It is critical that you don't buy links but instead attract other businesses to organically link to your website because of the quality of the content, relevancy and authority. Acquiring links that you didn't ask for is the nirvana of SEO. It's something that you should always be striving for and building towards over the long term. This is done by putting in the work to make your website link-worthy, whether that's through a great product or aspect of your service, or via producing great content that is referenced by other websites.

Alongside this long-term approach, you can also leverage a range of link-building techniques which allow you to build your authority and increase your chances of ranking well and getting traffic from organic search.

Social media can also help to a certain extent. By itself, social media is not necessary for ranking well on search engines, however, it provides a unique opportunity to reach customers and potential prospects.

When it comes to social media the best approach is to focus your efforts on engaging your customers with interesting content, promotions, polls and conversations that will increase their affinity for your brand. That's not to say you can't promote your website to a certain degree, but improvement in local rankings typically come from other factors.

Another type of Off-Page SEO is Local SEO. Local SEO is an especially critical component to your strategy if your business is locally oriented. For local businesses, part of the Off-Page SEO is really in-person SEO. Word-of-mouth marketing also plays a big role in getting people to your business. Happy customers can leave reviews online that Google and other potential customers can use to see how well you are doing.

As you can see, Off-Page SEO supplements On-Page SEO. Both go hand in hand. You need to focus on link-building, branding and appearance efforts to make the most of your SEO. You can optimize your site all you want, but if it isn't perceived as a quality destination for people, you won't rank well. Off-Page SEO is an integral part of your SEO strategy.

On the next page or a separate piece of paper, brainstorm ways to promote your content.

WAYS I AM PROMOTING MY CONTENT

1. _____

2. _____

3. _____

4. _____

5. _____

6. _____

7. _____

8. _____

9. _____

10. _____

11. _____

12. _____

13. _____

14. _____

15. _____

16. _____

17. _____

18. _____

19. _____

20. _____

21. _____

22. _____

23. _____

24. _____

25. _____

26. _____

27. _____

28. _____

29. _____

30. _____

31. _____

32. _____

33. _____

34. _____

35. _____

36._____

37. _____

38. _____

39. _____

40. _____

41. _____

42. _____

43. _____

44. _____

45. _____

46. _____

47. _____

48. _____

49. _____

50. _____

51. _____

52. _____

53. _____

54. _____

55. _____

CHAPTER 4
THE NON-TECHNICAL GUIDE TO TECHNICAL SEO

Rounding out the major types of SEO is Technical SEO. Technical SEO refers to website and server optimizations that make it easy for search engines to crawl and index content. The foundation of a search engine strategy starts with Technical SEO as it allows your website to be accessed by search engines so that customers can discover your content. The scope includes managing elements like Crawling, Indexing, Status Codes, Page Speed, Content, Site Structure, Mobile Usability, SSL, Structured Data, Migrations, and Rendering for website as you can see from the image below.

Technical SEO Checklist

- ✓ Mobile-friendly website
- ✓ SSL certificate
- ✓ XML Sitemap
- ✓ Website Speed
- ✓ Duplicate Content
- ✓ Enable AMP
- ✓ Schema Markup
- ✓ Hreflang tags
- ✓ Orphaned links
- ✓ Broken Links
- ✓ URL Structure
- ✓ Breadcrumb Menus
- ✓ Internal Links
- ✓ Image Alt Text
- ✓ Google Search Console

Another way to think of Technical SEO is that there are no issues with your website. By ensuring that your website is problem-free, Technical SEO clears the way for your content to thrive and organic search traffic to increase.

Below or a separate piece of paper, go through all of your web pages and see which, if any, have issues. Write them down and find solutions via search engines for them.

I have checked all the options below to ensure my website meets the standards of Technical SEO.

WEBSITE NAME: _____

❑ Mobile Friendly   ❑ SSL Certificate   ❑ XML Site Map

❑ Website Speed   ❑ Schema Markup ❑ No Duplicate Content

❑ No Broken Links ❑ Image Alt Text   ❑ Internal Links

WEBSITE NAME: _____

❑ Mobile Friendly   ❑ SSL Certificate   ❑ XML Site Map

❑ Website Speed   ❑ Schema Markup ❑ No Duplicate Content

❑ No Broken Links ❑ Image Alt Text   ❑ Internal Links

WEBSITE NAME: _____

❑ Mobile Friendly   ❑ SSL Certificate   ❑ XML Site Map

❑ Website Speed   ❑ Schema Markup ❑ No Duplicate Content

❑ No Broken Links ❑ Image Alt Text   ❑ Internal Links

CHAPTER 5
SOAR TO NEW HEIGHTS
WITH LINK-BUILDING

Within SEO, link-building plays an important role in driving organic traffic via search engines, especially in competitive industries. When combined with strong Technical SEO foundations, great On-Page SEO, excellent content, and a good user experience, link-building can be extremely effective at driving more organic traffic.

The need for quality, relevance, and authenticity has never been more important today. While low-quality, spammy link-building techniques can work, they shouldn't play a part in a strategy for an organization whose goal is building for long-term organic search success. Link-building is a part of great marketing, and the organizations that understand this are usually the ones that win long-term.

Link-building is the process of acquiring hyperlinks from other websites to your own. A hyperlink, simply called a link, is a way for users to navigate between pages on the Internet. Search engines use links to crawl the web. They will crawl the links between the individual pages on your website (internal linking), and they will crawl the links between entire websites (external linking).

Acquiring links that you didn't ask for is the ultimate goal of SEO link-building. It's always something that you should be striving for and building towards over the long term. You do this by putting in the work to make your website link-worthy, whether that's through a great product or aspect of your service, or via producing great content that is referenced by other websites.

You can also leverage a range of link-building techniques that allow you to build your authority as well as increase your chances of ranking well. Link-building takes time and, when done correctly, can take your SEO to a new level.

On the next page or a separate piece of paper, carefully plan out and write your link-building strategy.

MY LINK-BUILDING STRATEGY

_____

_____

_____

_____

_____

_____

_____

_____

_____

_____

_____

_____

_____

_____

_____

_____

_____

_____

_____

_____

CHAPTER 6
AVOID THESE MISTAKES WITH CONTENT MARKETING

Content marketing is one of the most powerful ways to grow your business this year and beyond. Although everyone has heard of content marketing, it can be confusing how to actually execute a strategy that will deliver big results.

You've done everything you can with your content but still aren't seeing results. How come? Well, there's a chance you may have made a mistake somewhere along the way. With over 250 million pieces of online content being created every single minute, your content marketing strategy has to be on point.

What do I mean by that? SEO content marketing focuses on producing keyword-targeted content that drives qualified traffic from Google to a company's website. Qualified traffic refers to visitors who are likely to find the content useful and relevant to their situation. In some cases, it may mean the visitors are ready to buy the company's product or service.

Content marketing and SEO increasingly go hand in hand. Even so, it's important to remember that SEO-focused content only really works when the brand or publisher creates content about topics related to its expertise and that pinpoints keywords that its target audience is searching for online.

Here are some common content marketing mistakes that companies are making and some tips on how to avoid them:

NOT CREATING REUSABLE CONTENT

You can reuse a blog post by taking the data from a piece of content and creating something else, such as an infographic or video, with some of the same information.

In basic terms, reusable content is content that can be republished in a different format or at a different time. This means that you can maximize content creation resources and improve your content marketing ROI.

While any piece of content has the potential for reuse, reusable content should be specifically designed for reuse. This means structuring and categorizing it in a way that makes it easy to find, reconfigure, and adapt at a later date.

Reusing content offers several benefits to content marketers. These benefits include:

- Reduced content development and maintenance costs
- Improved quality and consistency
- Potential to reach a wider audience

The first point is perhaps obvious. Rather than allocating budget and resources on a single piece of content, you can use these resources to create multiple pieces of content to publish in different places.

Reusing parts of content at later dates also means that reviewing and updating it regularly is naturally built into the content cycle. This constant reviewing and reusing of content means that quality and consistency naturally improve over time as a result.

NOT CREATING ENOUGH CONTENT

A common misconception is that you need to go out there and publish as much content as possible. The truth is that putting loads of content out there is not a great idea. It will not win you backlinks or rankings in the SERPs. It will only show your potential audience that your content is lacking in substance which isn't good for your content marketing efforts.

So, what can you do instead? Think quality over quantity. This is one of the easiest content marketing mistakes to avoid. Suppose you're having problems keeping a set schedule for your content. In that case, you can create what's known as an editorial calendar which is a visual workflow that helps with any content creation schedule issues by posting content on time.

EDITORIAL CALENDAR TEMPLATE

Content Title	Focused Keyword	Content Type	Publish Date	Owner(s)

NOT KNOWING YOUR AUDIENCE

Taking the time to create a customer avatar or customer persona can help you properly target the right audience with your content and understand your target market. Unfortunately, many businesses skip this step and just start creating content which can lead to businesses attracting leads that will never purchase. That's why understanding the search intent of your target audience is an important step.

Now, don't panic, it's not like you need to create a marketing plan for both the humans and the bots you're trying to reach with your next campaign. But, you can't develop meaningful, human-centered content without acknowledging the machines that your users will engage with first. Creating content for humans and machines is all about improving the user experience for everyone, no matter what technology they are engaging with. So, if you consider machines as you develop, structure, and publish content, you'll find you've produced better experiences and built better brand relationships with the humans you're looking to reach.

CREATING THE WRONG CONTENT

Doing only keyword-targeted content usually does not result in a good user experience. Human readers are unlikely to follow your content because instead of targeting reader interests, you are throwing out keyword-targeted content for the search engines. While your content needs to be read by search engines, you must write for your audience first. This is why you need to create personas and goes back to knowing your audience.

How well do you know your audience? If you answer is anything less than "so incredibly well" then you're likely missing out on reaching even more potential clients. Knowing exactly who you're marketing to can mean the difference between resonating with the people who need your services and turning them off completely and permanently.

Getting to know your clients or customers on this level helps you find what platforms they're hanging out on, use the right words to entice them and build campaigns they love.

NOT OPTIMIZING FOR SEARCH ENGINES

While creating content just for search engines is a mistake, you should also refrain from ignoring them completely. Search engines can drive continuous traffic to your site, and the more content you create, the more traffic can increase.

You should do some keyword research before you publish each article so that you can insert keywords into the title and meta tags. Ideally, your article should contain a mix of content designed to engage your audience and other thought leaders in your niche, plus designed to rank in the search engines.

NOT PROMOTING CONTENT

To maximize your reach, consider promoting your content on multiple channels or even repurposing it. Look for communities and social media platforms where you can share your content.

Build relationships with influencers by sharing their content and mentioning them in your articles. Participate in communities to get your name out there by visiting and contributing regularly to online groups and forums.

You should also consider using email outreach to share your content. Remember, you can always adjust your content marketing plan as you move forward, but be sure you at least have a plan in place when you start.

EXPECTING RESULTS TOO QUICKLY

This is the biggest mistake people make. How long should content marketing take before results are seen? While the amount of time and effort required to do well with content can vary, you should plan for content marketing to be a long-term strategy.

As the number of articles on your site increases, your content will rank for more search terms, attract more links and social shares, and website traffic will start to accelerate.

SELLING TOO MUCH

While adding a call to action (CTA) into your content can make sense in certain circumstances, some businesses make the mistake of selling too much in their content. Mentioning your company in every single blog post makes readers question your authenticity. Readers are more likely to follow or read content from sources they feel are genuinely providing the best, unbiased information.

BLINDLY FOLLOWING GENERIC CONTENT MARKETING ADVICE

Don't make the mistake of blindly "following the herd." To win at content marketing, you have to be able to make your judgments about what works and what doesn't. People who become thought leaders do so because they can form their own opinions and be creative instead of just following what everyone else is doing or saying.

NOT INVESTING IN THOUGHT LEADERSHIP

Achieving thought leadership in a niche is a content marketer's dream goal, but many businesses may get discouraged from pursuing this goal due to the amount of competition in this area. However, the significantly higher return on investment makes thought leadership a goal that content marketers should pursue.

If you want to win big with content marketing, then try guest blogging in your area of expertise. Content marketing is challenging, but with persistence and the right mindset, any business can grow through effective content creation.

Below or on a separate piece of paper, explore topics in your industry for ideas in content marketing.

THIS IS THE CONTENT I HAVE THAT CAN BE REUSED

_____

_____

_____

_____

_____

_____

_____

_____

_____

_____

_____

_____

_____

_____

_____

_____

_____

_____

THIS IS THE CONTENT I HAVE THAT NEEDS TO BE OF BETTER QUALITY

_____

_____

_____

_____

_____

_____

_____

_____

_____

_____

_____

_____

_____

_____

_____

_____

_____

_____

_____

_____

_____

HERE ARE THE DEMOGRAPHICS AND PSYCHOGRAPHICS OF MY AUDIENCE

_____

_____

_____

_____

_____

_____

_____

_____

_____

_____

_____

_____

_____

_____

_____

_____

_____

_____

_____

_____

_____

_____

I HAVE GONE THROUGH EACH PAGE OF MY WEBSITE(S) AND/OR BLOG(S) AND ALL OF MY CONTENT IS WRITTEN FOR HUMAN BEINGS AND NOT JUST SEARCH ENGINES

WEBSITE NAME: _____

❏ Page 1	❏ Page 2	❏ Page 3
❏ Page 4	❏ Page 5	❏ Page 6
❏ Page 7	❏ Page 8	❏ Page 9
❏ Page 10	❏ Page 11	❏ Page 12
❏ Page 13	❏ Page 14	❏ Page 15
❏ Page 16	❏ Page 17	❏ Page 18
❏ Page 19	❏ Page 20	❏ Page 21
❏ Page 22	❏ Page 23	❏ Page 24

CONTENT THAT NEEDS TO BE RE-WRITTEN

_____

_____

_____

_____

_____

_____

_____

_____

_____

_____

_____

_____

_____

_____

_____

_____

_____

_____

_____

_____

_____

BLOG NAME: _____❑ **OKAY**

WHAT NEEDS TO BE FIXED

_____

_____

_____

_____

_____

_____

_____

_____

_____

BLOG NAME: _____❑ **OKAY**

WHAT NEEDS TO BE FIXED

_____

_____

_____

_____

_____

_____

_____

_____

CHAPTER 7
HELPFUL CONTENT
UPDATE

SEO is constantly changing and that couldn't be clearer when on August 18, 2022, Google announced it would be adding a new factor to its rankings called Helpful Content Update. This update began rolling out the following week, however, the effects will be seen gradually as more data feeds the machine learning algorithm over time.

This is the first major Google update since the Core Web Vitals update was announced in May 2022. Broad Core updates are major, recurring algorithm improvements that Google makes that have wide, general scopes.

WHAT IS GOOGLE'S HELPFUL CONTENT UPDATE?

According to Google, this update to their search engine ranking algorithm is "part of a broader effort to ensure people see more original, helpful content written by people, for people, in search results," and "aims to better reward content where visitors feel they've had a satisfying experience, while content that doesn't meet a visitor's expectations won't perform as well."

This update is specifically targeted at content that is written for search engines first and people second. Google believes that SEO is a helpful activity when it's applied to "people-first content," but finds that content written primarily for search engine traffic is strongly correlated with content that searchers find unsatisfying. The following statement comes straight from Google . . .

> *"Any content — not just unhelpful content — on sites determined to have relatively high amounts of unhelpful content overall is less likely to perform well in Search, assuming there is other content elsewhere from the web that's better to display. For this reason, removing unhelpful content could help the rankings of your other content."*

This update introduces a new site-wide signal that Google will consider, along with other algorithm signals, any content that is deemed "unhelpful content" (i.e. search-engine first instead of people-first) will now be far less likely to perform well in search. If a majority of a site's content is not deemed valuable to users, then it's likely that the entire site's performance will suffer.

Google's systems will identify content that it deems "unhelpful" in an automated way using machine-learning models. Sites identified by this update may find their rankings will degrade over the course of several months.

The bottom line is that if you want your content to dominate the search engines, care about your audience and put in the effort to write for people. Demonstrate that you've formed a researched opinion, illustrate that you can communicate your opinion and engage audiences with compelling writing. And if you can't find someone who can do it for you because like SEO it's an investment in your business that will pay off in the long run.

HOW DOES THE HELPFUL CONTENT UPDATE DIFFER FROM OTHER GOOGLE SEARCH UPDATES?

Google's Helpful Content Update is a new organic search algorithm update and many are saying it's the most impactful update released since "Panda" back in 2011. Panda was an update designed to reduce the rankings for low-quality sites and shook up almost 12% of all queries. That may not seem like a lot but keep in mind that it's estimated Google handles 5.6 billion queries a day, so that percentage is nothing to sneeze at.

WHAT IS THE PURPOSE OF THE HELPFUL CONTENT UPDATE AND WHO WILL BE IMPACTED?

Google has said that AI-written content shouldn't be outpacing content written by people. In addition, content written with the intent for people shouldn't be outpaced by content written to game the system by way of structuring that content solely by what they think a search algorithm wants. In other words, don't try to game the algorithm. It won't work and your ranking will suffer.

How will Googlebot decipher what is written by a person and what is AI-written? That's a good question and has yet to be seen. In the past, there have been certain search updates that impacted specific industries and, with the context of this update's stated purpose, sites classified as YMYL (Your Money or Your Life) will most likely see the most impact. Google updated its quality rater guidelines recently to define what constitutes YMYL. You can find out more about YMYL in Chapter 34.

The big takeaway here is that this update will impact sites as a whole rather than specific pages of a site. So, if you have a website with three pages of great, original content and a thousand pages of canned content that's more-or-less filler, expect to feel some shockwaves from this update.

SHOULD YOU BE CONCERNED?

The bottom line is if you have a site (or multiple sites) that follows Google's best practices with unique content with the intent to serve the reader, there shouldn't be much to worry about.

As a reminder, here are Google SEO Best Practices when it comes to content.

1. Original and Unique Content
2. Engaging Content
3. Good Titles and Descriptions
4. Demonstrate Your Expertise
5. Score 100% When It Comes to On-Page SEO
6. NEVER Violate Google Webmaster Guidelines
7. Keep Your Website Fresh
8. Forget About Spammy Link-Building
9. Promote on Social Media
10. Stay In Sync with the Latest Trends

WHAT CAN YOU DO?

The best way to avoid issues with this update is to create a focused content strategy that assigns specific topics to specific pages. Don't put a bunch of ideas into one page. Use correct internal linking to connect related pages. Do it with logic and don't assign random pieces of unrelated text to be the anchor text. You may also want to check out our chapter on Pillar Pages and Topic Clusters.

On the next page or on a separate page, layout your Pillar Pages and Topic Clusters and then incorporate them into your website. This will take time and you don't want to rush the process. The first thing you want to do is go through your website and see what content you can use. Then decide if it qualifies as Pillar Page content or Topic Clusters.

EXISTING CONTENT ON MY WEBSITE THAT MEETS ALL OF GOOGLE'S GUIDELINES

1. _____

2. _____

3. _____

4. _____

5. _____

6. _____

7. _____

8. _____

9. _____

10. _____

11. _____

12. _____

13. _____

14. _____

15. _____

16. _____

17. _____

18. _____

19. _____

20. _____

21. _____

22. _____

EXISTING CONTENT ON MY WEBSITE THAT I CAN USE

1. _____

2. _____

3. _____

4. _____

5. _____

6. _____

7. _____

8. _____

9. _____

10. _____

11. _____

12. _____

13. _____

14. _____

15. _____

16. _____

17. _____

18. _____

19. _____

20. _____

21. _____

22. _____

EXISTING CONTENT ON MY WEBSITE THAT NEEDS TO BE DELETED

1. _____

2. _____

3. _____

4. _____

5. _____

6. _____

7. _____

8. _____

9. _____

10. _____

11. _____

12. _____

13. _____

14. _____

15. _____

16. _____

17. _____

18. _____

19. _____

20. _____

21. _____

22. _____

CHAPTER 8
PILLAR PAGES & TOPIC CLUSTERS: AN EVOLUTION IN SEO

As I've stated previously SEO is an ongoing process that requires you to stay ahead of the curve. To that end, this chapter talks about what Pillar Pages and Topic Clusters are, why they're important and how they improve your SEO. ***You still need to write quality content and use keywords.***

WHAT ARE PILLAR PAGES & TOPIC CLUSTERS?

Pillar Pages are content that provides a high-level of information on a broad topic, while linking to more specific content pieces. (ie: SEO, photography, real estate).

Pillar Pages typically don't contain in-depth or detailed content. Instead they cover many different aspects of a broad topic. For example, you might have a Pillar Page called Graphic Design. This page could contains sections on typography, layout, color, print and much more.

So why are Pillar Pages and Topic Clusters such a popular way to organize content? It's not just about SEO (although that's a big component). Here are 3 benefits of a well-executed Pillar Page strategy:

1. **Streamlined, Focused Content Ideation**. Some businesses come up with disjointed topics and ideas just to make sure they're churning out content. But that isn't a content strategy, and it's not sustainable, it's just churning out content for the sake of getting as much content out there as you can and that's a waste of valuable time.

Pillar Pages, on the other hand, give you a roadmap for your content ideas: You start with a broad, high-level topic and work your way out to more specific content. The best thing is you don't have to create new content for each Topic Cluster, just update and reuse relevant existing content

2. **SEO Improvements**. Here's a simple explanation of how Pillar Pages can give your site an SEO boost. Google understands how topics and sub-topics relate to each other, and uses those signals to analyze your site content and rank it in search results. By structuring your content into Topic Clusters and strategically linking between your Pillar Page and subtopic content, you can build your site's Expertise, Authority, and Trust (E-A-T). You'll learn more about this later in this workbook.

3. **Engaging Content.** Well-executed Pillar Pages and Topic Clusters make it easier for users to find the specific topics they're interested in and click through to learn more about them, keeping them on your site and building your authority in the process. Creating content like this increases your sites SEO, improves the user experience, and makes it more likely that site visitors will convert.

Remember good, quality content and SEO are ALL about the user experience. I may repeat this often in this workbook, but as long as your goal is about the user experience you can't go wrong.

The example on the next page shows how Pillar Pages and Topic Clusters work. As you can see, we start our main topic as the Pillar Page and have links going back and forth from the Pillar Page to Topic

Clusters. Then our Topic Clusters link to sub-topic pages that go into more detail.

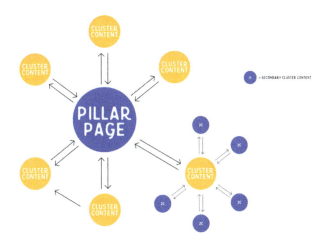

For the SEO component of a Topic Cluster to work, each of these content pieces should link back to the Pillar Page, and also link to other content in the cluster.

3 TYPES OF PILLAR PAGES

Now that we've explained what Pillar Pages are, here's more detail about them. Pillar Pages have 3 new categories:

1. **"What Is" Pillar Pages** are used to engage audiences. These are explanatory posts designed to help beginners learn about a particular topic. Examples include user searches for What is SEO? These users are likely to search sub-topics such as:

   a. What is Google Analytics?
   b. What is a keyword?
   c. What is anchor text?
   d. What is alt text?

3 Types of Pillar Pages That Rank

Pillar Page: Single, comprehensive, authoritative piece of content on a given topic

1. "What is X?"

- Define a product, category, discipline or industry
- Make a case for new tech
- Top of funnel (TOFU) education

Example:
What is a French Roast?
1. Definition
2. Why it matters
3. History
4. French vs Dark

2. "How To Y"

- Explain a process, your market needs
- Make a case for your solutions/philosophy
- Step by step tutorials

Example:
How To Steam Milk
Step 1: Lorem ipsum dolor sit amet, consectetur adipiscing elit, sed
Step 2: Lorem ipsum dolor sit amet, consectetur adipiscing elit, sed
Step 3: Lorem ipsum dolor sit amet, consectetur adipiscing elit, sed
Step 4: Lorem ipsum dolor sit amet, consectetur adipiscing elit, sed

3. "Best of Z?"

- List tips, tactics, facts
- Be competitive – Don't list obvious stuff
- Step by step tutorials

Example:
Top 10 Coffee Makers
1. Methodology
2. List

coffee maker image | Lorem ipsum dolor sit amet, consectetur adipiscing elit, sed

coffee maker image | Lorem ipsum dolor sit amet, consectetur adipiscing elit, sed

BELOW ARE IDEAS FOR "WHAT IS" PILLAR PAGES I WILL CREATE FOR MY WEBSITE

1. _____

2. _____

3. _____

4. _____

5. _____

6. _____

7. _____

8. _____

9. _____

10. _____

11. _____

12. _____

13. _____

14. _____

15. _____

16. _____

17. _____

18. _____

19. _____

20. _____

21. _____

22. _____

23. _____

24. _____

25. _____

26. _____

27. _____

28. _____

29. _____

30. _____

31. _____

32. _____

33. _____

34. _____

35. _____

2. **"How To" Pillar Pages** are where users can learn how to perform a particular task smoothly and efficiently. When a user visits your

website to find answers to their questions (otherwise known as queries), other queries naturally come up while searching for the information they originally asked for. This is a great opportunity for website owners to add Topic Clusters to answer the extra questions so that the user can keep reading without interruption. Examples of "How to" Pillar Pages include:

a. How to choose the right domain name?
b. How to find the perfect theme for your WordPress website?
c. How to add an SSL to your website?
d. How to integrate a WordPress theme on your website?

BELOW ARE IDEAS FOR "HOW TO" PILLAR PAGES I WILL CREATE FOR MY WEBSITE

1. _____

2. _____

3. _____

4. _____

5. _____

6. _____

7. _____

8. _____

9. _____

10. _____

11. _____

12. _____

13. _____

14. _____

15. _____

16. _____

17. _____

18. _____

19. _____

20. _____

21. _____

22. _____

23. _____

24. _____

25. _____

26. _____

27. _____

28. _____

29. _____

30. _____

31. _____

32. _____

33. _____

34. _____

35. _____

3. **"Ultimate Guide" Pillar Pages** are the final type of Pillar Pages on this list. Most people come to search engines looking for an answer to a

question. I'm sure you've come across a web page calling itself an "ultimate guide" for your answer. These web pages are helpful resources and they're meant to give more than just a quick answer to a question.

"Ultimate Guides" provide a huge value to the reader by covering details of a topic that are usually unimportant when looking for a straight and simple solution. The purpose of an ultimate guide depends on whether you're the reader or the writer of the article.

For readers, "Ultimate Guides" are more than just a blog post or simple review. Something calling itself an "Ultimate Guide" implies that the article covers details needed to help someone make a complex decision or build something more advanced than a simple blog post could cover.

Writers, however, create "Ultimate Guides" to help their audience, build authority, and create content that a search engine will recommend to others. "Ultimate Guides" are great for content marketing, sharing on social media, and evergreen content on a website.

BELOW ARE IDEAS FOR "ULTIMATE GUIDE" PILLAR PAGES I WILL CREATE FOR MY WEBSITE

1. _____

2. _____

3. _____

4. _____

5. _____

6. _____

7. _____

8. _____

9. _____

10. _____

11. _____

12. _____

13. _____

14. _____

15. _____

16. _____

17. _____

18. _____

19. _____

20. _____

21. _____

22. _____

23. _____

24. _____

25. _____

26. _____

27. _____

28. _____

29. _____

30. _____

31. _____

32. _____

33. _____

34. _____

35. _____

36. _____

37. _____

38. _____

39. _____

40. _____

41. _____

42. _____

43. _____

44. _____

45. _____

46. _____

47. _____

48. _____

49. _____

50. _____

podcasts.apple.com › us › podcast ⌄

Ultimate Guide to Partnering® on Apple Podcasts

5/5 ★ ★ ★ ★ ★ (79)

- How Sada Taps into The Power of Ecosystems to Drive Their Greatest Results. SADA's ISV & M...
- A MASTERCLASS Achieving Your Greatest Results Partnering with Google. Google's Ecosyste...
- Adam Michalski & Vince Menzione on What Makes an Ultimate Partnership? Vince Menzione, ...
- Google Transforms the Future of Healthcare and What it Means to You? Google's Healthcare L...

www.amazon.com › Ultimate-Guide-Aromatherapy ⌄

The Ultimate Guide to Aromatherapy: An Illustrated guide to ...

The Ultimate **Guide** to Aromatherapy INTRODUCTION . Everyone is talking about essential oils these days. You can find ample information on them from a variety of media sources that explore...

4.7/5 ★ ★ ★ ★ ⋆ (54)   **Author:** Jade Shutes, Amy Galper

Format: Paperback

www.ultimateguidetosoap.com › ⌄

HOME | Ultimate Guide to Hot Process Soap

The Ultimate **Guide** to Hot Process Soap covers everything you need to know about making your own soap at home. Whether you are interested in hot process, cold process, or liquid soap - the...

ignitevisibility.com › ultimate-guide ⌄

The Ultimate Guide to Creating Ultimate Guides

Oct 12, 2022 · Step 1: Create for Your Niche. Before creating your **guide,** consider the niche you want to build authority in. For instance, a link-building **guide** builds SEO authority, and a baking...

www.amazon.com › Ultimate-Guide-Google-Perry ⌄

Ultimate Guide to Google Ads: Marshall, Perry, Rhodes, Mike ...

Perry Marshall is one of the most expensive business strategists in the world. He is endorsed in FORBES and INC Magazine. At London's Royal Society, he announced the world's largest science...

4.7/5 ★ ★ ★ ★ ⋆ (196)   **Price:** $16.19

Brand: Entrepreneur Press   **Author:** Perry Marshall, Mike Rhodes, Bryan ...

WHAT ARE THE BENEFITS OF ADDING PILLAR PAGES TO YOUR WEBSITE?

Adding Pillar Pages to your website has a number of benefits including:

1. **Enhances the User Experience.** User experience is a priority for search engines and should be one for website owners to increase their SEO ranking. Having well-structured content with proper internal linking, search engine bots can easily crawl through your website. Using Pillar Pages and Topic Clusters can easily improve the user

experience as it allows users to easily navigate through web pages in a well-defined structure so they don't end up reaching irrelevant web pages.

2. **Longer Average Session.** Pillar Pages provide a lot of information in a single place so users can easily navigate from one topic to another as well as to sub-topics. By doing this, it encourages users to spend more time on your website resulting in longer average sessions.

When there's a lot of information available, users are likely to visit that information and less likely to bounce from your site to a competitors site.

3. **Promotes Search Engine Ranking.** Website owners face a lot of challenges to get their web pages ranked, however, Pillar Pages give your website a clean structure that makes it easier for search engine bots to crawl it. Poorly structured websites affect website rankings significantly and make it difficult for visitors and search engines to navigate a site, so adding Pillar Pages to your website is a win-win.

Below or on a separate page, lay out your Pillar Pages and Topic Clusters and then incorporate them into your website. This will take time and you don't want to rush the process.

PILLAR PAGE CONTENT

1. _____

2. _____

3. _____

4. _____

5. _____

6. _____

7. _____

8. _____

9. _____

10. _____

11. _____

12. _____

13. _____

14. _____

15. _____

16. _____

17. _____

18. _____

19. _____

20. _____

21. _____

22. _____

23. _____

24. _____

25. _____

26. _____

27. _____

28. _____

29. _____

30. _____

31. _____

32. _____

33. _____

34. _____

35. _____

36. _____

37. _____

38. _____

39. _____

40. _____

41. _____

42. _____

TOPIC CLUSTERS

1. _____

2. _____

3. _____

4. _____

5. _____

6. _____

7. _____

8. _____

9. _____

10. _____

11. _____

12. _____

13. _____

14. _____

15. _____

16. _____

17. _____

18. _____

19. _____

20. _____

21. _____

22. _____

23. _____

24. _____

25. _____

26. _____

27. _____

28. _____

29. _____

30. _____

31. _____

32. _____

33. _____

34. _____

35. _____

36. _____

37. _____

38. _____

39. _____

40. _____

41. _____

42. _____

CHAPTER 9
SOCIAL MEDIA & SEO: PERFECT TOGETHER

Do social media signals have a direct impact on search rankings? The truth is, it doesn't really matter. The reality is that social media plays a big role in helping companies get their content in front of a larger audience. That can lead to many things that benefit SEO, including more backlinks, improved engagement signals, and more owned SERP real estate for branded queries.

In addition, understanding both SEO and social media marketing help you perform better on both channels. Audience research on social media helps you create more targeted content. SEO research also helps you understand what your social audience wants to read.

So what is the relationship between social media and SEO? First off, success in both SEO and social media starts with great content. I'll say it again: **success in both SEO and social media starts with great content.** Social media is all about engaging with people. The more you do this, the more likely you'll be ranked higher because people and search engines will both love you.

Here are some SEO/Social Media marketing points to consider on how social affects SEO:

- Post useful materials on social media. Useful materials will help you gain traction, increase your content reach, and generate backlinks.
- Better information helps social media profiles rank in search results and gain traction (grow your followers and drive traffic).
- Quality helps build your brand community. You can also enhance your brand reputation.
- Links from social media can help Google with indexation of your blog/posts.
- Indexation can lead to more search traffic and improved rankings.

To maximize your reach, consider promoting your content on multiple platforms. Remember the social media platforms you want to be on are where your customers are not the ones you think you should or want to be on.

On the next page or a separate piece of paper, start sharing content that engages your audience because it helps boost social shares. Also, it makes it effortless for people to share your posts to strengthen those signals.

THIS IS MY ENGAGING CONTENT

_____

_____

_____

_____

_____

_____

_____

_____

_____

THIS CONTENT NEEDS TO BE MORE ENGAGING

_____

_____

_____

_____

_____

_____

_____

_____

_____

THIS IS MY PLAN FOR CREATING ENGAGING CONTENT

_____

_____

_____

_____

_____

_____

_____

_____

_____

_____

THIS IS MY PLAN FOR SHARING MY ENGAGING CONTENT

_____

_____

_____

_____

_____

_____

_____

_____

_____

CHAPTER 10
REVIEWS AND SEO: A POWERFUL COMBINATION

The relationship between customer reviews and SEO is vital to your brand's online reputation. Reviews don't just solidify the social proof needed for consumers to trust you and your services/products, they're also a necessary factor in increasing your exposure online.

Without reviews, you're not taking full advantage of the SEO benefits that can set you apart from the competition. It's safe to say that your online reviews and SEO plan won't be effective immediately, but it's never too late to start one. Getting the foundation built now ensures success down the road.

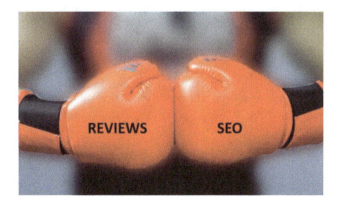

PROACTIVELY ASK FOR REVIEWS

Being able to ask for reviews also allows you to help meet some of the review factors for optimized search rankings. There are numerous ways to ask for reviews, including emails or SMS messages. Regardless of the method you choose, make sure that your request is short and to the point. If possible, personalize the message to make it more sincere.

RESPOND TO YOUR REVIEWS

With the reviews flowing in, your work is not done. You'll need to set aside time and create a review response plan. People want their voices heard and responding to their feedback shows that you're actively listening to them. This is especially true of negative reviews. Don't ignore them!

From an SEO standpoint, responding to reviews is another major search ranking factor. It tells Google that you're not just receiving feedback and turning a blind eye to what people are saying. It shows that you're actively monitoring your reputation and taking lessons from feedback to improve the customer experience.

Learning how to respond to negative reviews is an essential skill for any brand to have because of its impact on past and future customers. When done correctly, it allows you to tell your side of the story while finding a way to resolve the issue amicably and potentially bring back a customer. It also helps you save face in the eyes of those still deciding whether or not to purchase something from you, and how you handle yourself when dealing with negative feedback can be the deciding factor.

On the next page or a separate piece of paper, plan out how you will ask and respond to reviews, especially negative ones.

MY STRATEGY FOR ASKING FOR REVIEWS

_____

_____

_____

_____

_____

_____

_____

_____

_____

_____

_____

_____

_____

_____

_____

_____

_____

_____

_____

_____

_____

MY STRATEGY FOR RESPONDING TO NEGATIVE REVIEWS

_____

_____

_____

_____

_____

_____

_____

_____

_____

_____

_____

_____

_____

_____

_____

_____

_____

_____

_____

_____

CHAPTER 11
THE SYMBIOTIC RELATIONSHIP OF PODCASTS AND SEO

The symbiotic relationship between podcasts and SEO is a two-way street. When syndicated properly, podcasts can improve your brand reputation visibility and provide new opportunities to earn and generate links that boost your SEO strategy.

Conversely, organic traffic from your SEO strategy can bring more traffic and more listeners to your podcast. This is especially powerful if you're monetizing your podcast as a separate stream of revenue.

There are tactics you can use to optimize your podcast, for both written and audio content, so that it ranks higher within search engine results. This means not only more listeners for your podcasts, but also more website visitors and improved brand awareness. Some of these podcast SEO tips overlap with general SEO practices, while others are specific to audio content.

One of the most effective strategies to put you ahead of competitors is content marketing. Strategic use of content can help your site rank higher, both in terms of your domain and individual site pages. This content can be blogs posts, infographics, and of course, podcasts. Content marketing goes hand in hand with SEO, driving more inbound traffic to your episodes.

Here are some other podcast strategies you can try:

1. Pick podcast keywords for every episode. This is one of the most important podcast SEO tips we found through our research. Using the right keywords is essential for SEO of any kind, and podcasts are no exception. Keywords tell Google that your episode is relevant to a user's search, and therefore make it more likely to be featured in results.

2. Use the keywords in your episodes. Now that Google has integrated indexing of audio content, this means that podcasts can appear in search results. This is a great opportunity as episodes may turn up in any search, not just when users are specifically looking for podcasts.

3. Include written content for each podcast episode. This is another key way to optimize your podcast yet many podcasters don't bother. They simply upload a new episode to their podcast host and expect listeners to appear. It doesn't work that way.

4. Google and other search engines easily scan written text to decide whether your content is relevant. By giving Google some written content to read to complement the audio content, it has more of a chance of ranking an episode in search results.

PODCAST STATISTICS

Here is a list of key podcast statistics and it is growing by leaps and bounds.

1. There are 383.7 million podcast listeners globally.
2. As of June 2022, there are over 2.4 million podcasts with over 66 million episodes between them.
3. The United States has the most podcast listeners. It is predicted that there are over 100 million active podcast listeners in the US.
4. Scandinavian countries have the highest podcast penetration rate.
5. One-third of the American population listens to podcasts regularly
6. Smart speaker sales increased by 22% during the pandemic, and it is one of the most popular channels to listen to podcasts.
7. 78% of the US population is aware of podcasts. Out of which, 28% listen to podcasts weekly.
8. 160 million US citizens have listened to podcasts at least once.
9. 91% of Australian people are aware of podcasts.

On the next page or a separate piece of paper, make a list of related, local podcasts and write out a script that you will use to get on.

EXISTING PODCASTS THAT I CAN CREATE PARTNERSHIPS WITH

_____

_____

_____

_____

_____

_____

_____

_____

_____

_____

_____

_____

_____

_____

_____

_____

_____

_____

_____

_____

_____

CHAPTER 12
THE SEO BENEFITS OF PODCASTING

Merely producing podcast episodes and distributing them to an audience isn't going to increase your domain authority or improve your SEO, however, below are some advantages and opportunities of podcasting.

- One of the reasons podcasting has become so popular is its friendliness to newcomers. The audio format and ease of publication means you won't have to invest much time or money to get started, yet the potential audience you can build with a podcast is practically unlimited in size and when compared to other link-building strategies, can actively increase your ROI.

- Using certain sites, your podcast episodes can be syndicated across numerous high-authority websites. And more importantly, many of the syndicated links are 'DoFollow', which means the links provide some SEO juice.
- Podcasts are typically hosted by one or two people who serve as the leads for the show. If you're trying to fit your podcasting strategy with your SEO campaign, it's ideal to have your primary guest authors as your podcast hosts.
- Podcasting is also a fantastic gateway for relationship building and collaborative content development. By networking with other podcasters, conducting interviews, and guest hosting on other podcasts, you'll expand your network of content collaborators and partners. As a side effect, you'll trade links with a wider range of industry authorities, and you'll open the door to more co-author and co-publication deals.
- You can also consider your podcast as an alternative social media channel. Just as you might syndicate and popularize your best content through channels like Facebook and Twitter, you can talk about your best content on a podcast, increasing its visibility and capacity to earn links.

For a podcast to benefit your SEO strategy, link-building strategy, and brand reputation, you need to adhere to these important podcasting fundamentals:

- **Invest in quality equipment.** Your podcast will only be listenable if you invest in decent equipment. That doesn't mean you have to go out and buy the most expensive microphone on the market, but you should at least strive for mid-range territory.
- **Differentiate from the competition.** The topic of your podcast needs to be something that stands out. There are already a million podcasts about general education, politics, comedy, and marketing, so what makes yours different?

- **Speak as an expert.** People want a podcast host who knows what they're talking about. Make sure you come across as an expert in whatever field you try to cover.
- **Market and support your work.** Even the best podcast would fail to generate an audience without ample support. It's critical to market your podcast to new audiences and go out of your way to get attention for it. Link-building is the best way to approach this.
- **Engage.** People like to listen to podcasts because it makes them feel like they're a part of something. If you want them to get the warm and fuzzies when they listen to you, you have to engage with them. Just like in social media, the more engaging you are, the more loyal your followers will be.

Part of the power of podcasting rests with its ability to manifest in multiple forms. Take advantage of this by syndicating your podcast in audio, video, and written transcript form. You can offer all varieties on each episode page on your main site while also taking advantage of separate platforms like YouTube.

Like everything else in this workbook, podcasting is not easy, and you need a plan. Sometimes it helps to first be a guest on someone else's podcast. That's what I'm doing.

On the next page or on a separate piece of paper, research which podcasts work for your industry. Create a plan or strategy to incorporate a podcast into your SEO strategy. It might mean being a guest on a few podcasts before investing in the equipment. The important thing is to have a plan so that when the time comes, you are prepared to incorporate podcasting into your SEO strategy.

MY PLAN TO CREATE PARTNERSHIPS WITH RELEVANT PODCASTS

_____

_____

_____

_____

_____

_____

_____

_____

_____

_____

_____

_____

_____

_____

_____

_____

_____

_____

_____

_____

_____

CHAPTER 13
ROLLING TO SUCCESS WITH MOBILE RESPONSIVENESS

It's no secret that mobile internet use is more popular than ever. Over 50% of web pages are served to mobile phones, and the number steadily grows each year. The numbers shouldn't be surprising if you think about your own habits. Many of us even search Google from our phones while looking at a computer screen. How crazy is that?

Because of the internet's shift from desktop-centric to mobile-centric, having a responsive design is more important than ever. Once you understand how the mobile responsive web benefits SEO and other digital marketing efforts, you'll realize why it's crazy not to focus on your mobile site. Now that doesn't mean you need 2 separate sites. Most website software allow for content to resize automatically depending on the screen size. If you do your own HTML coding for websites then you need to be sure you have the following at the beginning of your code.

```
<!DOCTYPE html>
<html lang="en">
<head>
<meta charset="UTF-8">
<meta http-equiv="X-UA-Compatible" content="IE=edge">
<meta name="viewport" content="width=device-width, initial-
scale=1">
```
[THIS IS THE CODE THAT TELLS THE WEBSITE TO ADJUST DEPENDING ON THE SCREEN SIZE]
```
<title>Untitled Document</title>
```

It's important to remember that unlike most things in the world of technology, mobile internet use is **NOT** just a trend. Almost everyone has a smartphone, and tablets are routinely being used everywhere from elementary schools to retirement homes. Sometimes, I think babies are born knowing how to use mobile devices.

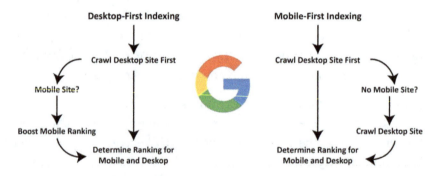

Mobile responsiveness is one of the few things that Google has directly confirmed are given priority in search. Google recognizes that mobile versions of websites are now the primary version. Search engines are all about delivering helpful content, and a site that doesn't work for over half of all web users is far from helpful if you're on a phone. To respond to this, Google gives significant ranking boosts to pages that are mobile responsive.

While mobile users usually have shorter visit durations and see fewer pages, they account for about 50% of total E-commerce revenue. Most importantly, with the introduction of Mobile-First indexing, the relevance of your site is determined largely by your mobile appearance. If you have a poor user experience, hidden content, or tiny text, you could see a significant drop in your desktop rankings too.

So how does Mobile-First Indexing impact SEO? That's a great question, and I'm glad you asked. Mobile-First basically means that your mobile site is the first thing that Google includes in their index and acts as a baseline for determining rankings. It is important to note that this doesn't mean your site is **only** indexed on mobile. You can expect Google to crawl your site on a desktop as well.

Here are some ways that a responsive website benefits SEO and your overall digital marketing efforts.

1. Mobile Responsiveness
2. Website Usability
3. Faster Page Loading
4. Lower Bounce Rate
5. Increased Social Shares
6. No Duplicate Content

Even though most, if not all, websites are responsive at this point, I felt it was important to include Mobile Responsiveness here since it affects your rankings.

On the next page or a separate piece of paper, go through all of your web pages, blogs, and other content to ensure that it all looks good on mobile devices from a user experience perspective.

CHECK ALL YOUR WEB PAGES/BLOGS AND OTHER CONTENT
TO ENSURE ALL THESE FACTORS ARE PRESENT

Web Page/Blog/Content _____

❑ Mobile Responsive   ❑ Website Usability   ❑ Website Speed

❑ Lower Bounce Rate   ❑ Increased Social Shares

❑ No Duplicate Content

Web Page/Blog/Content _____

❑ Mobile Responsive   ❑ Website Usability   ❑ Website Speed

❑ Lower Bounce Rate   ❑ Increased Social Shares

❑ No Duplicate Content

Web Page/Blog/Content _____

❑ Mobile Responsive   ❑ Website Usability   ❑ Website Speed

❑ Lower Bounce Rate   ❑ Increased Social Shares

❑ No Duplicate Content

Web Page/Blog/Content _____

❑ Mobile Responsive   ❑ Website Usability   ❑ Website Speed

❑ Lower Bounce Rate   ❑ Increased Social Shares

❑ No Duplicate Content

Web Page/Blog/Content _____

❑ Mobile Responsive   ❑ Website Usability   ❑ Website Speed

❑ Lower Bounce Rate   ❑ Increased Social Shares

❑ No Duplicate Content

Web Page/Blog/Content _____

❑ Mobile Responsive   ❑ Website Usability   ❑ Website Speed

❑ Lower Bounce Rate   ❑ Increased Social Shares

❑ No Duplicate Content

Web Page/Blog/Content _____

❑ Mobile Responsive   ❑ Website Usability   ❑ Website Speed

❑ Lower Bounce Rate   ❑ Increased Social Shares

❑ No Duplicate Content

Web Page/Blog/Content _____

❑ Mobile Responsive   ❑ Website Usability   ❑ Website Speed

❑ Lower Bounce Rate   ❑ Increased Social Shares

❑ No Duplicate Content

Web Page/Blog/Content _____

❑ Mobile Responsive   ❑ Website Usability   ❑ Website Speed

❑ Lower Bounce Rate   ❑ Increased Social Shares

❑ No Duplicate Content

CHAPTER 14
SETTING UP SUCCESS WITH YOUR SITE ARCHITECTURE

Google sends its bots or search spiders to virtually all websites regularly to crawl and index new web pages. However, these spiders need help to know new and updated pages are on your website.

And this is where a simple and well-laid-out site structure and architecture come in play. You should have a simple and clear site structure if you want your pages to get crawled and indexed fast. This simple rule has never changed, and you must make sure your site architecture is set up correctly.

Well Optimized Site Architecture

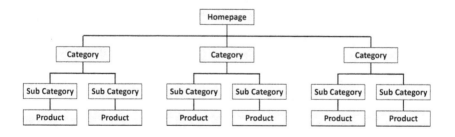

There are four main components of site structure you should work on to help bots in the crawling task.

1. HTTPS

The right website structure starts with an appropriate HTTPS or Hypertext Transfer Protocol. The only SEO-friendly way to do this is to use a secure protocol. This is because Google announced in 2014 that it had added HTTPS as one of its ranking factors. This is a rare event since most of Google's ranking algorithms have been kept secret, and all the factors listed online are assumptions, although backed by facts.

Therefore, having your website on the secure HTTPS will enable you to rank better. HTTPS also adds a level of protection and security to your website and brings other benefits that relate to site analytics too. In addition, HTTP sites now come up with a warning that the site is unsecure and basically you proceed at your own risk.

I HAVE CHECKED THE EXPIRATION DATE OF MY SSL CERTIFICATE

WEBSITE NAME _____

❏ SSL Certificate (Expiration Date _____)

2. BREADCRUMBS

A breadcrumb is a type of navigation that shows the location of a user on your website. The name came from Hansel and Gretel's fairy tale, whereby they left breadcrumbs on their way into the woods to be able to locate their way back. Breadcrumbs present your website hierarchy and indicate where your visitor is. This minimizes the number of actions a visitor takes if they need to go back to different sections of your site.

If your website has a comprehensive hierarchy and different sections that call for a clear structure, you need breadcrumbs. These are also recommended for E-commerce websites with different products.

However, they should not replace primary navigation guided by your internal page linking.

3. URL STRUCTURE

A savvy site structure should have a user-friendly and consistent URL structure. The URLs describe the pages for both search engines and users. Therefore, make them brief and descriptive. Ideally, a user should understand your page content based on its URL. You can add the primary keyword to the URL to strengthen the relevancy of your pages and help search engines understand your web pages better. What's more, you should separate words in your URLs with hyphens.

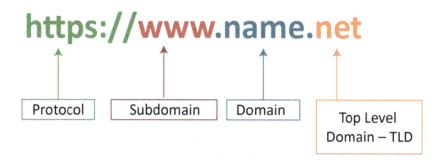

When choosing whether to use .net, .com, .org and .edu, you can choose a domain name from any of these extensions to make a website, however these extensions were created to distinguish between different types of websites. The truth is most people don't know which of these are best for their website(s). Here is the purpose of each type of domain

The .com extension is generally intended for commercial businesses. This is by far the most popular and commonly used TLD (top level domain), as most people are creating websites because they are starting businesses.

The .net extension represents "network". It is recommended and suitable for the internet, email and networking service providers. The

.org extension means organization and is typically used by non-profit organizations.

The. .edu extension stands for education, but I'll bet you knew that one. This is typically used for universities, colleges and educational sites. And of course, the .gov extension is used for the government.

We always recommend choosing a .com domain name. While it can be tempting to come up with clever blog names using new extensions, **.com is still the most established and credible domain name extension.** This extension is one of the most chosen extensions since with this extension your website also starts ranking well in the search engines.

Web Page _____

URL Structure _____

_____

Web Page _____

URL Structure _____

_____

Web Page _____

URL Structure _____

_____

Web Page _____

URL Structure _____

_____

Web Page _____

URL Structure _____

_____

Web Page _____

URL Structure _____

_____

Web Page _____

URL Structure _____

_____

Web Page _____

URL Structure _____

_____

Web Page _____

URL Structure _____

_____

Web Page _____

URL Structure _____

_____

Web Page _____

URL Structure _____

_____

Web Page _____

URL Structure _____

_____

Web Page _____

URL Structure _____

_____

Web Page _____

URL Structure _____

_____

Web Page _____

URL Structure _____

_____

4. SILO CONTENT

'Siloing' content means defining the hierarchy of pages on your website. In other words, it is how your pages interlink. Internal links help to improve your website visibility by linking newer posts with older ones. You need to categorize your web pages and always ensure the pages within one category are linked. This ensures your user can navigate from one resource on your site to another without having to take many actions. Internal links help to pass SEO juice to all the connected pages on your website.

While a site architecture is typically created before your website is created, on the next page or a separate piece of paper, based on the information presented here, lay out a site architecture for your website.

Home Page
(Index Page)

Silo Pages
(Site Index)

Categories
(Content)

Supporting Pages
(Content)

BELOW OR ON A SEPARATE PAGE CREATE YOUR SITE'S ARCHITECTURE

_____

_____

_____

_____

_____

_____

_____

_____

_____

_____

_____

_____

_____

_____

_____

_____

_____

_____

_____

_____

_____

CHAPTER 15
STRUCTURED DATA MARK-UP OR STRUCTURED DATA-RICH SNIPPET

Structured data has become one of the biggest factors in search. Since Schema.org was launched in 2011 by search giants Google, Bing, and Yahoo as an initiative to create a common set of schemas for the web, there have been many improvements in the database.

The number of websites using structured data is small even though the advantages of it are clear. Google and other search engines have made better ways to track data and advocate its use of it. Specifically, Google made better use of structured data through Rich Snippets to optimize the appearance of search results.

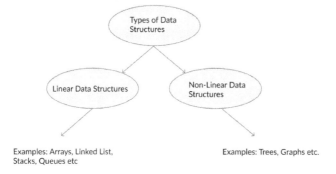

Examples: Arrays, Linked List, Stacks, Queues etc

Examples: Trees, Graphs etc.

The structured data markup that is placed on a web page allows Google and other search engines to better understand the content of a page. This results in "Rich Snippets" or "Rich Results." These search results have extra information based on the structured data of a webpage. This adds extra interaction for the user.

Rich snippets are important to SEO because they make normal search results much more attractive and interactive for users. It gives users a "taste" of how your actual page content looks, which makes them more likely to click.

Even though structured data is not a direct ranking factor, adding structured data to your pages and optimizing it for rich snippets is undoubtedly helpful. It can be quite intimidating for non-web developers, but Google has created a number of resources for webmasters to make it easier to understand.

Again this is a more advanced subject and is best left to those who have made it their business to understand structured data. If you want to try it yourself, then I strongly recommend you backup your website before trying the more advanced strategies in this workbook.

The table below shows all the different types of structured data that can be added to your site today. These categories are examples of all the types of data that Google will use to generate rich snippets.

Content Type	Available Features	Notes
Articles	Top stories carousel	The Top stories carousel requires sthat your content be published in AMP. For more information, see AMP with Structired data.
	Rich results	
Local Businesses	Place actions	Requires explicit opt-in. Express interest.
Music	Music actions	Requires explicit opt-in. Express interest.
Recipes	Rich results	
	Host-specific lists	
Reviews	Critic review cards	Requires explicit opt-in. Express interest.
TV & Movies	Watch actions	Requires explicit opt-in. Express interest.
Videos	Rich results	

CHAPTER 16
XML SITEMAPS

Imagine trying to find a place you've never been without a map or any instructions. Getting there would be pretty tricky, right? You might be surprised to learn that search engines suffer from the same problem. Thankfully, there's a way to put a map in their hands and point them in the right direction with a tool called XML sitemaps.

So, just what are XML sitemaps, and what is their significance for SEO? Do you need to create one for your website? A sitemap is a list of all of your website URLs. A sitemap's job is to tell search engine crawlers what they should look at on your site.

To understand what an XML sitemap is, you need to first know how search engines find pages. They use bots, otherwise known as crawlers, to probe the web and find relevant results to search query. As someone who has used a search engine many times in your life, I'm certain you have experienced these crawlers being pretty good at quickly finding the websites that provided the information you were seeking.

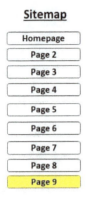

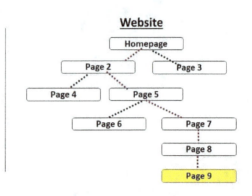

An XML sitemap is essentially a text file that describes all the URLs on a website. When created correctly, it makes for more efficient crawling, which means that search engines can find your pages quicker. XML sitemaps help keep search engines updated on changes to your website, most notably when you add a new page or remove an old one.

Sitemaps also may have extra info on each URL, for example when they were last updated, their importance, and if other versions exist in different languages. It's important to keep in mind that creating an XML sitemap provides no guarantee that search engines will crawl and index your page. However, having one is an excellent way to increase your chances, especially if your navigation or internal linking strategy doesn't link to all of your pages.

Okay, so now the $25,000 question. Do I need to have a sitemap? The answer is no. However, competition among websites is fierce these days, and unfortunately, SEO often falls short when it comes to outranking competitors. Interestingly enough, you probably won't come across XML sitemaps on a list of SEO best practices. Yet savvy website owners are now turning to them as a way to rank higher in search engines. and that's because they help ensure that a website ranks accurately on the results page. Since XML sitemaps serve to enhance website ranking, they can also improve other SEO efforts and your website becomes visible to a greater number of users, which increases traffic to your page.

The best part about this roundabout SEO strategy is that all major search engines recognize sitemaps, which means you only have to do the legwork once. Using them for indexing is where they come in handy. As mentioned before, the vast amount of content on the World Wide Web sometimes slows search engines down. Even though they're more than capable of finding pages without a sitemap, this tool speeds up the crawling process.

BELOW OR A SEPARATE PAGE CREATE YOUR OWN SITEMAP FOR YOUR WEBSITE

CHAPTER 17
UP YOUR SEO GAME
WITH IMAGES

Whether you're writing articles for a blog, an online magazine, or just writing content for your website, chances are you'll find yourself asking whether your text needs an image or not. The answer is always "Yes." Images bring an article to life and also contribute to your website's SEO.

Images, when used correctly, will help readers better understand your article. Remember the old saying "A picture is worth a thousand words?" Well it might not apply to Google, but it's certainly true when you need to spice up 1,000 dull words, illustrate what you mean in a chart or data flow diagram, or just make your social media posts more enticing. Remember 90% of our communication is visual. In addition images help those who are disabled which is something you need to consider especially since businesses (small and large) are being sued because people who are disabled don't have access to your website. That is a topic for another time, however, I wanted to at least bring it up here. On the next page is an example of what search engines see when looking at websites.

It's a simple recommendation: add images to every article you write to make them more appealing. What's more, since visual search is becominging increasingly important it could provide you with a nice bit of traffic. And if you have visual content it makes sense to put image SEO a bit higher on your to-do list. There are a few things to keep in mind when using images.

Any images used on a page should be properly optimized. Otherwise, search engines can't understand what they represent. Things like optimizing the filename, file size, and ALT text are critical for image SEO. Default filenames are your enemy as they tell Google nothing about your content. After all, it's just a bunch of numbers and letters that offer no real information or meaning.

The way to fix this is to rename your file something that means something. What does that really mean? Tell Google what's in your image. Be very descriptive to get your point across. Remember that Google is a blind robot that can't see your image. Google reads your image file names to make sense of the content. For example, if your image is a blue leather purse with tassels, then it wouldn't be a bad idea to name your filename "blue-leather-purse-with-tassels." It's that simple. Keep in mind, however, that you want to use your (relevant) keywords here, use hyphens and make it short.

On the next page or on a separate page, go through ALL of your images and make sure they have names that identify them.

USE THIS CHECKLIST TO ENSURE ALL OF YOUR IMAGES COMPLY WITH GOOLGE'S GUIDELINES

Image _____

❏ Correct Filename   ❏ Add Image Structured Data

❏ Relevant Keywords   ❏ Scaled Images   ❏ Optimized Images

❏ Added Alt Tags   ❏ Correct Format   ❏ Mobile Responsive

❏ Reduced File Size

Image _____

❏ Correct Filename   ❏ Add Image Structured Data

❏ Relevant Keywords   ❏ Scaled Images   ❏ Optimized Images

❏ Added Alt Tags   ❏ Correct Format   ❏ Mobile Responsive

❏ Reduced File Size

Image _____

❏ Correct Filename   ❏ Add Image Structured Data

❏ Relevant Keywords   ❏ Scaled Images   ❏ Optimized Images

❏ Added Alt Tags   ❏ Correct Format   ❏ Mobile Responsive

❏ Reduced File Size

Image _____

❏ Correct Filename   ❏ Add Image Structured Data

❏ Relevant Keywords   ❏ Scaled Images   ❏ Optimized Images

❏ Added Alt Tags   ❏ Correct Format   ❏ Mobile Responsive

❏ Reduced File Size

OPTIMIZING YOUR IMAGES AND WHY IT'S IMPORTANT

Image Optimization is the process of making the file size of your images smaller while preserving their quality and vibrance so they still look great on your website or wherever else you are using them.

There are two main aspects of image optimization. The first involves resizing images while maintaining quality, and the second involves optimizing the images for search engines with relevant keywords.

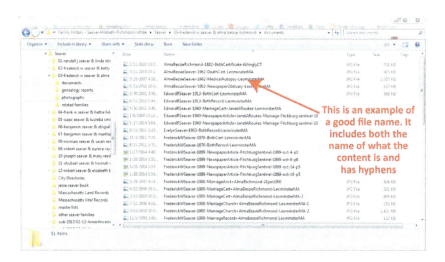

This is an example of a good file name. It includes both the name of what the content is and has hyphens

WHY IMAGE OPTIMIZATION IS IMPORTANT

The answer is an improved user experience. When the file size of your image is greatly reduced, your website's pages can load much faster and this results in a much better experience for your visitors. Keep in mind the following:

Page Loading Speed is Now a Search Ranking Factor. It is now widely known that Google and other search engines are using web Page Loading Speed as one of their ranking factors, and making sure your images are optimized is an important part of that.

User Experience. When your website takes forever to load, it doesn't exactly provide the best experience for your users. Your users expect your site to load quickly. Optimizing your images helps to ensure a better user experience and that you meet users' expectations.

May Improve Website Conversion Goals. The bottom line is it doesn't matter what your goal is; whether it's having your visitors stay on your site longer, make a purchase or another goal having fast loading pages is extremely important. The faster and easier to navigate your site is, the more it is that people will stick around longer.

SEO. Image optimization will help to ensure that your images rank in image searches on Google, and it will also be beneficial to the overall SEO (search engine optimization) of your website. Additionally, page speed plays an important part in Google's search algorithm, and image optimization will help you avoid the organic search penalties of having a slow website.

CHAPTER 18
RAMP UP YOUR TITLE TAGS

A title tag is an HTML tag that is written <title> and is placed under the <head> section in the source code of your website. It labels your page for both people and search engines. In SERPs, titles appear as the blue text that people click to navigate to your page. They also appear at the top of browser tabs.

Title tags tend to span no more than 60 characters, although it depends on the search engine and the width of the letter combinations. If a title exceeds the display length, the search engine cuts it off, and users can't see the whole title.

Title tags provide a context on what the subject matter of the page is. While it has little impact on organic rankings, missing, duplicate, or poorly written title tags can negatively impact your SEO. As you can see from the image on the next page, our title tag meets all the guidelines, as shown by the green bar below it in Yoast SEO.

SEO title

SEO – Marketing – Design We Get Results

SEO – Marketing – Design We Get Results

Title tags are important for 2 main reasons:

1. Users will see your title tag in the SERP. Depending on the quality of your title tag and meta description, they may choose to pass your page by or click on it to find out more.
2. Google is also checking out your title tags. It's only one element they use when determining what a page is about. A well optimized title tag can improve your rankings.

Adding and optimizing a title tag whenever you publish is not particularly time-consuming, but failing to do so can have strong negative effects on your site.

It's easy to get so caught up with keywords and word counts that you forget real people are also reading this title and deciding if they want to read your content based on it. Your title should be readable, clear, and eye-catching. When possible, use emotional appeals and demonstrate the value of your product or service. Think about your word choice and the emotions you're evoking. You want a title that will jump out and grab the attention of your readers.

Here are 3 Ways to Optimize Your SEO Title Tags:

1. Use Branding When Appropriate

Title tags can be a great place to add the name of your company or other branded terms. This is really important on key pages such as your homepage. For other pages, you can add branding if it fits.

2. Use Separators

In order to fit the important stuff in without going over the character count, you should put the important information in the beginning of the title tag. To pack it all in while staying concise, you can use punctuation such as commas, dashes, pipes, and colons to separate parts of your title.

3. Be Accurate

Google will sometimes rewrite your title tag if they think the title and the content are a mismatch. So, it's recommended that you honor the actual content on your page. Readers are also more likely to bounce quickly if they discover your content is a far cry from their expectations.

Below on the next page or a separate piece of paper, write out a few title tags for your web page or blog

Web Page _____

Title Tag _____

Web Page _____

Title Tag _____

Web Page _____

Title Tag _____

Web Page _____

Title Tag _____

Web Page _____

Title Tag _____

Web Page _____

Title Tag _____

Web Page _____

Title Tag _____

Web Page _____

Title Tag _____

Web Page _____

Title Tag _____

Web Page _____

Title Tag _____

Web Page _____

Title Tag _____

Web Page _____

Title Tag _____

Web Page _____

Title Tag _____

Web Page _____

Title Tag _____

Web Page _____

Title Tag _____

Web Page _____

Title Tag _____

Web Page _____

Title Tag _____

Web Page _____

Title Tag _____

CHAPTER 19
ARE YOUR META DESCRIPTIONS GETTING THE JOB DONE?

Meta descriptions describe what the page is about. This is often displayed in the SERPs underneath the title of the page. Just like the title of a book catches your attention, a page's meta tag is the first step that invites people to click on your page in the Search Engine Results Pages (SERPs).

Optimizing meta descriptions correctly can help improve:

- Click through rate (CTR)
- Perception of the quality of the result
- Perception of what your website offers

Meta descriptions are typically 120 characters. If you use more than that, your text will be truncated with 3 dots (…), indicating more text is available. People want to find the information they need quickly, so it's best not to have your meta description truncated.

Rich snippets can technically be any length. It's best to keep rich snippets long enough that they're sufficiently descriptive, so we recommend descriptions between 50 and 160 characters. Keep in mind that the "optimal" length will vary depending on the situation, and your primary goal should be to provide value and drive clicks.

WHY ARE META DESCRIPTIONS IMPORTANT FOR SEO? DO META DESCRIPTIONS AFFECT SEARCH RANKINGS?

Yes and no. Google announced in September of 2009 that neither meta descriptions nor meta keywords factor into Google's ranking algorithms for web search.

The meta description can, however, impact a page's click-through rate (CTR) in Google SERPs, which can positively impact a page's ability to rank. These short paragraphs are the webmaster's opportunity to "advertise" content to searchers, and the searcher's chance to decide whether the content is likely to be relevant to their query and contain the information they're seeking.

Because meta descriptions have an indirect impact on search rankings and especially because they can significantly impact user behavior, it's important to put some effort into writing them.

Meta description

CJ Design & Consulting gets results with SEO, Marketing or Design. We can do it for you. We can show you how to do it.

Aug 22, 2021 — CJ Design & Consulting gets results with SEO, Marketing or Design. We can do it for you. We can show you how to do it.

On the next page or a separate piece of paper, write out a few meta descriptions for your web page or blog.

Web Page _____

Meta Description _____

_____

Web Page _____

Meta Description _____

_____

Web Page _____

Meta Description _____

_____

Web Page _____

Meta Description _____

_____

Web Page _____

Meta Description _____

_____

Web Page _____

Meta Description _____

_____

Web Page _____

Meta Description _____

_____

Web Page _____

Meta Description _____

_____

Web Page _____

Meta Description _____

_____

Web Page _____

Meta Description _____

_____

Web Page _____

Meta Description _____

_____

Web Page _____

Meta Description _____

_____

CHAPTER 20
DO YOU DISTINGUISH YOUR HEADER TAGS FROM OTHER TAGS?

HTML header tags are used to differentiate the headings (h1) and sub-headings (h2-h6) of a page from the rest of the content. These tags are also known to webmasters as heading or header tags. The most important heading tag is the h1 tag, and the least important is the h6 tag.

Header tags can directly impact your rankings by:

- Making your content easier to read
- Providing keyword-rich content about your content for search engines.

This is Heading 1

This is Heading 2

This is Heading 3

This is Heading 4

This is Heading 5

This is Heading 6

In HTML coding, the heading tags from h1 to h6 form a top-down hierarchy. This means that if you skip any of the tag numbers, the heading structure will be broken, which is not ideal for On-Page SEO.

Header tags also make your pages more relevant. Google sees the text used within the HTML header tags as more valuable or a higher priority than the rest of the text on a page. Therefore, words used in the header tags are weighted more highly when Google is trying to determine if a page is relevant to a user's query. In fact, a page's h1 tag is one of the most important places to use a keyword.

For example, if your site is introduced with an h1 tag followed by an h3 tag, the hierarchy will be broken, meaning the heading structure is not as SEO-friendly. Ideally, every page should have an h1 tag but no more than one.

Below, on the next page or a separate piece of paper, identify your h1, h2, h3, h4, h5, & h6 tags for each page on your website(s) or blog(s).

Web Page _____

Header Tags:

H1 _____
H2 _____
H3 _____
H4 _____
H5 _____
H6 _____

Web Page _____

Header Tags:

    H1 _____
    H2 _____
    H3 _____
    H4 _____
    H5 _____
    H6 _____

Web Page _____

Header Tags:

    H1 _____
    H2 _____
    H3 _____
    H4 _____
    H5 _____
    H6 _____

Web Page _____

Header Tags:

    H1 _____
    H2 _____
    H3 _____
    H4 _____
    H5 _____
    H6 _____

Web Page _____

Header Tags:

    H1 _____
    H2 _____
    H3 _____
    H4 _____
    H5 _____
    H6 _____

Web Page _____

Header Tags:

    H1 _____
    H2 _____
    H3 _____
    H4 _____
    H5 _____
    H6 _____

Web Page _____

Header Tags:

    H1 _____
    H2 _____
    H3 _____
    H4 _____
    H5 _____
    H6 _____

CHAPTER 21
ARE YOUR HEADLINES COMPELLING ENOUGH?

Compelling headlines help your website content perform well on search. Word count is a key SEO factor for headlines. Long headlines don't appear in Google search results, and short headlines don't provide enough context for readers. Google prefers headlines that are 4-7 words long. Here are some other guidelines to keep in mind.

- Get to the point
- How will your reader benefit pain avoidance.
- Make it personal
- Curiosity

Adding sections and subsections with appropriate headers divides content into scannable blocks that are much easier to consume for both humans and bots. Look at your page's HTML header tags as a way of creating an outline or sketch of your article, using body content to fill in details and examples.

On the next page are examples of SEO-friendly headlines.

Headline Examples

HOW TO [ACHIEVE SOMETHING]	THE TRUTH ABOUT [SOMETHING]	DO YOU SUFFER FROM [PROBLEM] WHEN [SPECIFIC SITUATION]?
How to Become a Successful Blogger in 180 miutes.	The Truth About Online Marketing [Your Agency Won't Tell You]	Are You Sweating Bullets When Your Article Is Due?

# WAYS TO [ACHIEVE SOMETHING]	# MISTAKES THAT [CAUSE A NEGATIVE]	IMPROVE [SOMETHING] IN A [SPECIFIC TIME PERIOD]
10 Ways to Write a Headline that Captures Your Readers	7 Common Blogging Mistakes That Repel Readers	Go From Clueless to Killer With Your Blogging in 5 Days

SIGNS YOUR [YOUR SOMETHING IS BAD]	THE SECRET FOR GETTING [RESULT]	[ACHIEVE RESULT] WITH THE MOST EFFECTIVE WAY [TO DO SOMETHING]
Obvious Signs Your Website Fails to Attract and Convert Prospects	The Secret to Building Authority Through Your Blog	Double Your Social Share With the Most Effective Headline Templates

THIS, THAT, AND THE POINT OF THE STORY
Daydreams, Smelling Salts, and the Blog Posts that Inspire Readers

Now it's your turn. Below on the next page or on a separate piece of paper, write down some headlines for each of your web pages/blog posts keeping in mind the guidelines shared above.

ARE YOUR HEADLINES COMPELLING ENOUGH?

Web Page _____

Headline _____

Web Page _____

Headline _____

Web Page _____

Headline _____

Web Page _____

Headline _____

Web Page _____

Headline _____

Web Page _____

Headline _____

Web Page _____

Headline _____

Web Page _____

Headline _____

Web Page _____

Headline _____

Web Page _____

Headline _____

Web Page _____

Headline _____

Web Page _____

Headline _____

Web Page _____

Headline _____

Web Page _____

Headline _____

Web Page _____

Headline _____

Web Page _____

Headline _____

Web Page _____

Headline _____

Web Page _____

Headline _____

Web Page _____

Headline _____

Web Page _____

Headline _____

CHAPTER 22
IT'S NOT ALL ABOUT KEYWORDS BUT THEY ARE IMPORTANT

Keyword research is part of SEO (search engine optimization). It's the work someone does to come up with an extensive list of keywords they would like a website to rank for. To obtain this list, website owners need to dig into their desired audience and search engines. This is why knowing your audience is extremely important. What search terms do people type into Google when looking for a particular product, service, business or type of organization? And what do they expect to find? With this list, website owners can create content that will attract more high-quality traffic to their site. Keyword Research is never finished. It is essential to do it regularly.

The power of keyword research lies in better understanding your target market and how they are searching for your content, services, or products. Keyword research provides you with specific search data that can help you answer questions like:

- What are people searching for?
- How many people are searching for it?
- In what format do they want that information?

Before you perform any keyword research, you need to ask questions. Before you can help a business grow through search engine optimization, you first have to understand who they are, who their customers are, and what their goals are.

This is where corners are often cut. Too many people bypass this crucial planning step because keyword research takes time, and why spend the time when you already know what you want to rank for? The answer is that what you want to rank for and what your audience actually wants are often two very different things.

There are some concepts you need to know before you do any keyword research:

Head Keywords: also called "head terms" in SEO, are a big part of maximizing your organic traffic while also staying competitive compared to other websites. They can be popular search keywords that have a lot of search volume because they represent a broad topic or a well-known concept. Head keywords can be extremely short searches, even consisting of just one word.

Focus Keywords: a word or phrase you want a certain page on your site to be found for in Google. These are determined by doing your keyword research.

Long-Tail Keywords: are more specific and less commonly searched for than head keywords. Long-tail keywords focus on a niche. The longer and more specific search terms are the easier it will be able to rank for them since there is less competition. The logic behind using long-tail keywords is that even though there are less people searching for these terms, the people searching for them might be more motivated to buy, subscribe, sign up or take whatever action you want them to do. It works!

Search Intent: Search intent is _why_ people are searching. You don't ask a question for no reason, but the why really changes the type of answer you're looking for. Search intent matters because it's a key ranking factor. In fact, without it, everything else you're doing won't quite hit the sweet spot. Here are the 4 types of search intent.

- **Informational:** when a user wants to know something rather than buy.
- **Navigational:** when a user knows where it wants to go. It could be location-based or contain a brand keyword
- **Commercial:** when a user indicates an interest in buying, but never needs more information before they make a decision.
- **Transactional:** when a user is ready to take some kind of action. It could be to buy a product or sign up for a service.

10 STEPS TO DOING KEYWORD RESEARCH

1. Think about your mission and determine your SEO goals
2. Make a list of keywords you think people might search for
3. Research the keywords you've come up with
4. Use your research to find long-tail variants of your keywords
5. Analyze your competition for those keywords
6. Take a closer look at search intent for each keyword
7. Determine a keyword strategy – which keywords will you target?
8. Create optimized landing pages for your keywords
9. Evaluate if your keyword strategy is working and keep improving
10. Refresh your keyword research and your content regularly

UNCOVERING SEARCH VOLUME

The higher the search volume for a given keyword or keyword phrase, the more work is typically required to achieve higher rankings and the greater the competition. This is often referred to as keyword difficulty and occasionally incorporates SERP features. For example, if many SERP features (like featured snippets, knowledge graph, carousels, etc) are clogging up a keyword's result page, the difficulty will increase.

Big brands often take up the top 10 results for high-volume keywords, so if you're just starting out on the web and going after the same keywords, the uphill battle for ranking can take years of effort.

Below is an image showing the search volume of keywords related to SEO.

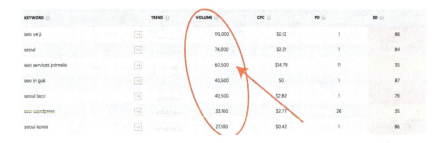

Go too low, though, and you risk not drawing any searchers to your site. In many cases, it may be most advantageous to target highly specific, lower competition search terms. In SEO, we call those long-tail keywords.

UNDERSTANDING THE LONG TAIL KEYWORD

It's wonderful to deal with keywords that have 50,000 searches a month, or even 5,000 searches a month, but in reality, these popular search terms only make up a fraction of all searches performed on the web. In fact, keywords with very high search volumes may even indicate ambiguous intent, which, if you target these terms, could put you at risk for drawing visitors to your site whose goals don't match the content your page provides.

Once you understand your target audience better, you can use tools such as Moz, Ubersuggest, SEMRush or Ahrefs to find specific keywords. Be sure to include the long-tail keywords and look at their search volume.

On the next page or a separate piece of paper, write down some long-tail keywords/keyphrases for each page of your website or blog. Remember that keyword/keyphrases that are longer and more specific are what visitors are more likely to use. They also typically have lower search volume than short or "head" keywords.

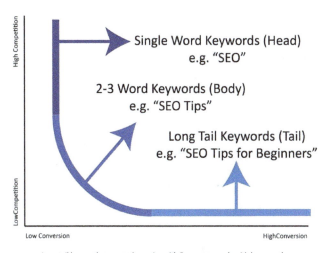

Long tail keywords are search queries with 3 or more words with low search
voume & competition levels yet have higher conversion rates

The next few pages are for brainstorming Head, Focus and Long-Tail Keywords I can use.

HEAD	FOCUS	LONG-TAIL

HEAD	FOCUS	LONG-TAIL
_____	_____	_____
_____	_____	_____
_____	_____	_____
_____	_____	_____
_____	_____	_____
_____	_____	_____
_____	_____	_____
_____	_____	_____
_____	_____	_____
_____	_____	_____
_____	_____	_____
_____	_____	_____
_____	_____	_____
_____	_____	_____
_____	_____	_____
_____	_____	_____
_____	_____	_____
_____	_____	_____
_____	_____	_____
_____	_____	_____
_____	_____	_____
_____	_____	_____
_____	_____	_____
_____	_____	_____
_____	_____	_____
_____	_____	_____
_____	_____	_____
_____	_____	_____
_____	_____	_____
_____	_____	_____
_____	_____	_____
_____	_____	_____
_____	_____	_____
_____	_____	_____
_____	_____	_____

CHAPTER 23
HOW TO RUIN YOUR RANKING WITH KEYWORD CANNIBALIZATION

Keyword cannibalization means having various blog posts or articles on your site that can rank for the same search query in Google. This is either because the topic they cover is too similar or because you optimized them for the same keyword. If you optimize posts or articles for similar search queries, they're eating away at each other's chances to rank. Usually, Google will only show 1 or 2 results from the same domain in the search results for a specific query. If you're a high authority domain, you might get 3.

Why is keyword cannibalism bad for SEO? If you cannibalize your own keywords, you compete with yourself for ranking in Google. Let's say you have two posts on the exact same topic. In that case, Google can't distinguish which article should rank highest for a certain query. In addition, important factors like backlinks and CTRs get diluted over several posts instead of one. As a result, they'll all probably rank lower. But, keyword cannibalism can also occur if you optimize posts for focus keywords that are not exactly but almost the same.

The solution is to merge or combine articles. If two articles attract the same audience and basically tell the same story, you should combine them. Rewrite the two posts into one amazing post which will help your rankings. Google loves lengthy and well-written content, and this will solve your keyword cannibalization problem. It's a win-win.

Below, on the next page or a separate piece of paper, check whether or not your site suffers from keyword cannibalization. The way you do that is to search your site for any specific keyword you suspect might have multiple results.

THESE WEB PAGES/BLOGS SUFFER FROM KEYWORD CANNIBALIZATION AND WILL BE FIXED

Web Page _____

Cannibalized Keywords _____

_____

_____

Web Page _____

Cannibalized Keywords _____

_____

_____

Web Page _____

Cannibalized Keywords _____

_____

_____

Web Page _____

Cannibalized Keywords _____

_____

_____

Web Page _____

Cannibalized Keywords _____

_____

_____

Web Page _____

Cannibalized Keywords _____

_____

_____

Web Page _____

Cannibalized Keywords _____

_____

_____

Web Page _____

Cannibalized Keywords _____

_____

_____

Web Page _____

Cannibalized Keywords _____

_____

_____

Web Page _____

Cannibalized Keywords _____

_____

_____

THIS IS MY STRATEGY FOR AVOIDING FUTURE KEYWORD CANNIBALIZATION

_____

_____

_____

_____

_____

_____

_____

_____

CHAPTER 24
OPTIMIZING YOUR SEO WRITING

Today, more than 90% of online experiences start with search engines. When people search keywords and phrases related to your business, you want to appear at the top of the Search Engine Results Pages (SERPs). To rank at the top, you need quality SEO-optimized content.

By optimizing a website for certain keywords, businesses can improve their visibility and organic search results within popular search engines like Google. In an age where most consumers begin their product searches online, SEO is essential for any business looking to attract new customers and grow their brand. Without fresh, quality content, search engines have nothing to rank in search results. SEO writing is crucial if you want to earn top rankings for search results related to your business.

70% of search engine traffic never goes past the first page of results. As a result, businesses that rank on the first page get 70% of the potential customers. If you invest in high-quality writing, you can strategically use keywords to create the type of content you need to attract high search volumes and organic traffic.

WHAT IS SEO-FRIENDLY CONTENT WRITING?

SEO-friendly content is mainly written to increase rank for a specific subject or multiple keywords. SEO content can either be a blog post, product page, video, how-to tutorial, list, infographic, glossary, or some other type.

Instead of writing ordinary content, you should specifically write search engine optimized content because SEO content can deliver value to your website and help you improve its visibility to potential customers.

Organic traffic delivers value to your website, and business owners are looking for the most effective methods to increase organic traffic. Search engines such as Google tend to pay more attention to websites with quality and search engine-optimized content.

If you ignore getting organic traffic, you will lose the ability to attract new customers. This is a loss to your business, and you will also have to spend money on getting organic traffic through ads.

Below, on the next page or a separate piece of paper, start writing SEO content for your web pages. Remember to include your keywords, but write for people, not just search engines.

Web Page _____

Optimized for the following Keyword _____

Web Page _____

Optimized for the following Keyword _____

Web Page _____

Optimized for the following Keyword _____

Web Page _____

Optimized for the following Keyword _____

Web Page _____

Optimized for the following Keyword _____

Web Page _____

Optimized for the following Keyword _____

Web Page _____

Optimized for the following Keyword _____

Web Page _____

Optimized for the following Keyword _____

Web Page _____

Optimized for the following Keyword _____

Web Page _____

Optimized for the following Keyword _____

Web Page _____

Optimized for the following Keyword _____

Web Page _____

Optimized for the following Keyword _____

Web Page _____

Optimized for the following Keyword _____

Web Page _____

Optimized for the following Keyword _____

Web Page _____

Optimized for the following Keyword _____

Web Page _____

Optimized for the following Keyword _____

Web Page _____

Optimized for the following Keyword _____

Web Page _____

Optimized for the following Keyword _____

Web Page _____

Optimized for the following Keyword _____

Web Page _____

Optimized for the following Keyword _____

Web Page _____

Optimized for the following Keyword _____

Web Page _____

Optimized for the following Keyword _____

Web Page _____

Optimized for the following Keyword _____

CHAPTER 25
HOW IS THE QUALITY OF YOUR SEO CONTENT?

SEO content is a subset of On-Page SEO. It is all about the quality of the content and how to make it better. This is a very important SEO success factor, so publishing great content that users love and search engines can understand is the winning combination.

I've been asked by many people countless times how do you know content is high quality? Well, here are 5 elements of quality content for SEO content writing.

1. Quality content satisfies the reader's intent. Before I even begin writing my article or blog, my first question is "who is going to be reading this and what do they want to know?" As mentioned earlier in this workbook, "intent" is a big factor in SEO content writing. That's why it's so important to know your audience and craft personas. It's a lot of work but trust me it's worth it. Writing quality content is not easy so aside from creating your personas, Google your topic and SEO search term(s), review the top-ranking pages in the search results and then figure out how to do better than those pages.

2. Quality content has "authority." I'll get more into authority later in this workbook when we get to the chapter on E-A-T. Google recently updated their algorithm to include authority as a ranking factor. For SEO content writing, this means you should focus on topics that are closely related to your website's subject matter and purpose. For example, I write on SEO, Content Marketing, Website Design, Graphic Design & Social Media Marketing because those are areas I know my stuff.

3. Quality content is comprehensive. Typically, longer content outperforms shorter content in rankings. But how long is long enough? My website is in WordPress and I use Yoast SEO, which I recommend and that plug-in guides me on how long my web pages and blogs need to be.

4. If you're not using WordPress and/or don't want the Yoast SEO plug-in there are other ways to find out this information, much of which will come from your analytics.

5. Quality content is easy to read. So now we have a dilemma of which I have experienced. Comprehensive content is good because it can answer a lot of the questions for searchers, but most people don't want to spend a lot of time reading to find the answer they want. That's especially true when people are on mobile devices.

So what do you do? Write as concisely as possible, Make sure you structure your content and design for easy readability by:

1. Using headings to introduce new topics
2. Break up long sections with subheading, bullets, indents & bold. Much of which I've done in this workbook.
3. Break up long paragraphs and use short sentences
4. Avoid passive voice wherever possible
5. Minimize jargon

6. Quality content includes engaging visuals. I already discussed the importance of using images in your articles, blog and on your website. I said it before but it bears repeating. 90% of human communication is visual. Break up long pages with visuals that reinforce your ideas, These visuals include:

1. Photos
2. Drawings
3. Icons
4. Infographics
5. Videos

Go through all of your content and compare it against the checklist on the next page.

Web Page/Blog/Content_____
❑ My content satisfies the reader's attention
❑ My content has authority
❑ My content is comprehensive
❑ My content is easy to read
❑ My content has engaging visuals

Web Page/Blog/Content_____
❑ My content satisfies the reader's attention
❑ My content has authority
❑ My content is comprehensive
❑ My content is easy to read
❑ My content has engaging visuals

Web Page/Blog/Content_____
❑ My content satisfies the reader's attention
❑ My content has authority
❑ My content is comprehensive
❑ My content is easy to read
❑ My content has engaging visuals

There are many more factors that need to be considered when it comes to determining if your content is of high quality, but let's start with these.

BELOW IS THE CONTENT THAT'S NOT QUALITY CONTENT (EITHER FIX OR REMOVE)

_____

_____

_____

_____

_____

_____

_____

_____

_____

_____

_____

_____

_____

_____

_____

_____

_____

_____

_____

_____

_____

_____

_____

CHAPTER 26
IMPROVE YOUR LOCAL SEO RANKINGS

With so much to consider regarding Google ranking factors, it's easy to become overwhelmed. Local SEO is a complicated task that requires ongoing upkeep in many different areas. You can't simply optimize your Google Business Page listing and expect to land in the local pack overnight.

What is local pack in SEO? Awesome question, thanks for asking. The Local Pack is a SERP feature that appears on the first page of results for any search query with a local intent. It features a map of business locations along with listings for three businesses relevant to a particular search.

SEO FOR LOCAL & SMALL BUSINESSES

Local SEO focuses on the geographic component of SEO, mainly targeting users who are searching locally for goods or services. With a local search, the search has two components: an industry and a location. Google has gotten really good at understanding the intent behind searches, especially those for local goods or services. So many local searches take the shape of "best bakery near me" or "local plumber."

While these terms don't always have a specific location, such as online & work from home businesses, Google is able to pinpoint the user's area and provides results that are close to the user. How amazing is that? With location services available on many mobile devices, Google does an incredible job of narrowing results for local queries to within a few feet of a user. Local intent will also take the form of inquiries about the type of business, phone number, hours of operation, driving directions, coupons and special offers, and especially ratings and reviews.

Local and organic SEO differ in specific ways, although local SEO benefits from organic SEO, especially for small businesses. Organic SEO utilizes a number of different strategies for a site to rank higher in search engine results pages and generally gain a higher domain score than their competition with Google.

Local SEO, while benefiting from the strategies for organic SEO, uses a number of other online strategies in order to capture local users. These include ranking in search engines, like Google and Bing, appearing in business directories like Yelp and Google Business Page. For local businesses, the power of local SEO is held primarily by business directories and online reviews.

Online reviews are considered one of the most important parts of local SEO since 86% of consumers read online reviews before visiting a business, and 91% of 18-34 year old consumers trust them as much as personal recommendations. As you can see, online reviews are a huge asset to small businesses, especially with websites like Yelp and Google making it extremely easy for businesses to set up their own pages for reviews and business information.

USE THE CHECKLIST BELOW TO ENSURE YOU ARE AVAILING YOURSELF OF EVERY LOCAL SEO OPTION.

CHECKLIST FOR LOCAL SEO

❏ Make sure that you have your business name, address, and contact details on all website pages.

❏ Add the Local Business schema on your homepage

❏ Create a Google Business Page Account

❏ Register your business with trusted directories such as Yelp, Yahoo, etc.

❏ Promote your website on local directories and websites (for example, online local newspapers).

I AM NOT TAKING FULL ADVANTAGE OF LOCAL SEO & HERE IS MY PLAN TO CHANGE THAT

_____

_____

_____

_____

_____

_____

_____

_____

_____

_____

_____

_____

_____

_____

_____

_____

_____

_____

_____

_____

_____

_____

_____

_____

_____

_____

CHAPTER 27

8 LOCAL SEO SEARCH FACTORS

There are many more local search ranking factors that Google takes into account, but outlined here are those that are the most important, as well as those that you actively have control over.

ON-PAGE SEO

When optimizing for local SEO, the best place to start is with the content on your website. Content quality is one of the most important Google ranking factors, as this makes your website more relevant and better serves your users.

Start with making sure that the content on your website is well written, helpful, and relevant to your keywords. While it's important to include them on your website, make sure to use keywords naturally. Don't stuff keywords into your content, as that will negatively affect you. In addition, make sure that your address and phone number are featured on every page of your website.

GOOGLE BUSINESS PAGE

One of the most important local search ranking factors is your Google Business. Page (GBP) listing. I can't tell you how many customers, prospects, and other business owners don't know they have a GBP listing, or they tell me that Google did it for them, and they can't get Google to make changes. Here's a little secret. You don't need Google to make changes for you. You can do it.

The first step is to claim your listing. Ensure your business name, address, and phone number are correct. This is useful not just for customers but also because the proximity of the business to the searcher is one of Google's main local ranking factors.

Complete your GMB listing as fully as possible, ensuring that you have selected the most appropriate category and included relevant keywords within your title and description as this will help optimize it. Check that your business hours are correct and that the link to your company website is current. Add your logo and some high-quality photos to improve your business' appearance in the local pack or Google Maps.

BACKLINK PROFILE

One of the biggest areas of local SEO that you should pay attention to is your backlink profile. More links doesn't necessarily mean better rankings. Google values only high-quality, relevant links, and any shady-looking ones can have a drastic result on your rankings. Outbound links are also considered, and exchanging links with relevant local businesses can help improve your rankings.

REVIEWS

This is another one of the important local SEO ranking factors that Google uses to determine how well you rank. Remember that Google Maps and the local pack show an overview of your business' reviews, so focus on getting good reviews from happy customers.

It's never okay to use fake reviews to boost your online presence or to reward people for leaving a positive review. Ask clients to leave you a review at the end of their purchase, and you'll be surprised at how quickly you get results. People want to help you and they need your help to do it. So don't be afraid of asking for reviews.

ONLINE CITATIONS

Wherever your business is mentioned online, ensure that your business name, address, and telephone number are correct and that they match the information on your website. If the address on your website says "123 Example Street" but your Yelp listing says "121-123 Example Road," then this can confuse things.

BEHAVIORAL SIGNALS

Google is more inclined to serve your site in the SERPs if it has a reputation for being helpful. The more people who interact with you, the higher up in the rankings you will appear. A great way to boost your behavioral signals is by optimizing your website for local SEO.

SEARCH PERSONALIZATION

Search personalization was introduced more than a decade ago to provide the most relevant results for an individual. In fact, "near me" is one of the most popular search terms. While some generic results will be the same regardless of who is searching, factors such as physical location will influence the rest of the results.

SOCIAL MEDIA

The high domain authority and user base of social sites like LinkedIn, Twitter, Facebook, and Instagram mean that Google pays close attention to them. If you search for any company name, you'll probably find their social media pages and their website at the top of the SERPs.

If people are talking about your brand on social media, this will feed into your rankings. Remember that Google's algorithms are smart enough to know whether these mentions are positive or negative, so monitor them and engage with your audience to preserve your reputation.

Below, on the next page or a separate piece of paper, ensure that you are following each of the factors mentioned.

ON-PAGE SEO

_____

_____

_____

_____

GOOGLE BUSINESS PAGE

_____

_____

_____

_____

BACKLINK PROFILE

_____

_____

_____

_____

REVIEWS

_____

_____

_____

_____

ONLINE CITATIONS

_____

_____

_____

_____

BEHAVIORAL SIGNALS

_____

_____

_____

_____

SEARCH PERSONALIZATION

_____

_____

_____

_____

SOCIAL MEDIA

_____

_____

_____

_____

CHAPTER 28
MAKE THE MOST OF YOUR MOBILE SEO

WHAT IS MOBILE SEO?

Mobile SEO provides search engine optimization of websites with a unique viewing on smartphones and tablets. The main goal is to achieve optimized content with a better ranking.

This effort will **drastically** improve both your Search Engine Results Pages (SERPs) rankings and your site's organic traffic. The users location, the device's operating system, and the screen size will all impact the quality of your Mobile SEO.

WHY IS MOBILE SEO IMPORTANT?

Mobile SEO is important because it ensures that mobile visitors have a good user experience that's optimized for their mobile device. Important factors of mobile search engine optimization include site design, site structure, page speed, and On-Page Mobile SEO practices.

According to Google, "When people have a negative brand experience on mobile, they are over 60% less likely to purchase from that brand in the future than if they have a positive experience." Google also reports that "some people are spending up to 70% of their time on mobile" and "mobile conversion rates are 47% of the levels achieved on desktop." In case you weren't aware of this already, Google now uses Mobile-First indexing, where it uses the mobile version of the content for indexing and ranking.

HOW MOBILE SEO IS DIFFERENT

Optimizing for mobile devices requires many of the same best practices of desktop SEO, but mobile search results are much more variable than desktop searches, because they are influenced by an additional set of factors.

Things like page organization, user location, operating system & screen size are among the top ranking factors. The interaction of these variables means that search engine crawling, indexing, and ranking processes differ between devices. Mobile SEO succeeds on any device and it may interest you to know that Google doesn't considers tablets to be mobile devices.

Here are the differences between desktop and mobile:

1. Search Engine Results Pages (SERPs)

What differs most between Desktop and Mobile SEO is the layout of the SERPs. Because mobile phones are smaller than desktop screens, Google doesn't have enough room for 2 columns. This means that anything on the right side of a desktop search result will stack above or below the organic search results, and fewer results will show on the first page—this is especially true for paid listings (pay-per-click results).

2. Location

Most modern mobile phones have a global positioning system (GPS), which provides search engines with more accurate location data than stationary desktop computers. Even if a device doesn't have a GPS, mobile phones have other ways of giving search engines location data, which influences search results.

This is one of the primary reasons that mobile search results are much more variable than desktop search results—if you search something in Bangkok, the results will likely be very different than if you search while in New York City. However, desktop searches are also influenced by the physical location of your mobile phone if you're logged into a Google account on both.

3. Screen Size

Google adapts search results to fit the device that you are using to search. This impacts how many results are visible on the page. When tablets came to the market they added even more variations to SERP layouts.

There are many other factors that make mobile SEO different from desktop SEO. The important thing is to ensure your website, blog, app or whatever is mobile friendly.

HOW DOES MOBILE SEO WORK?

Mobile SEO works by optimizing a website and content to achieve higher rankings in search engine results pages (SERPs). It works to improve organic traffic, which is traffic coming to a site from the SERPs. Google primarily crawls and indexes pages with its smartphone agent.

Because of Mobile-First indexing, the mobile version of your website is considered the primary version for crawling and organic SEO ranking purposes. If your mobile and desktop versions are the same, then you shouldn't have any problems with your site's performance in the search results. However, if your mobile site has different content than your desktop site, then you could experience ranking complications with SEO.

HOW TO IMPROVE YOUR MOBILE SEO

1. Use a Responsive Design

Google recommends responsive designs for mobile SEO purposes as dynamic serving websites require you to maintain multiple custom pages and multiple sets of content, The easiest way to improve your mobile SEO is to use a responsive design on your website. With a responsive design, your site has one URL and all pages share the same content for both the mobile version and desktop version.

Responsive design is better than dynamic serving or a separate domain because it's easier for Google to understand the content and index it accordingly. Dynamic serving uses server-side technology to serve a different version of your site to mobile users. The URLs stay the same but the files sent are completely different.

A separate domain usually refers to a subdomain with an "m." attached to the domain and it has different content on it. When a user visits your website from a mobile device, the server can detect this and serve the subdomain content instead of the standard content. Google supports separate domains but only if you make the correct connections between your regular desktop domain and the mobile domain, which is a lot more work.

In the "old days", we had to create two different websites: one for the desktop and the other for mobile. Typically the mobile site didn't have as much information as the "full website." Technology has come a long way and as long as you have the correct code for responsive design there should be no problems. The following code allows for the adjustment on the website based on the device being used. <meta name="viewport" content="width=device-width, initial-scale=1">

As you can see a lot is involved in using dynamic serving and a separate domain. It's much simpler to use responsive design and most if not all hosting companies offer responsive design.

2. Improve Your Mobile Site Speed

Speed is now a ranking factor for Google, so you must pay attention to it for mobile search engine optimization. This started in July 2017 when Google announced that page speed was a ranking factor for the mobile search index. Then, in May 2021, Google launched Core Web Vitals to capture the end-user experience. These and other factors are part of the Page Experience that falls under Core Web Vitals.

The other two important factors for mobile search engine optimization include:

- **LCP (Largest Contentful Paint):** This measures the amount of time it takes for the largest element of a requested page to appear in the viewport. A higher score (i.e. faster speed) gives the impression to a user that a page loads faster. Sites should strive for an LCP of 2.5 seconds or less.

- **FID (First Input Delay):** This measures the time from when a user first interacts with an element on your site to when the browser responds to that input. Examples include clicking a link or tapping a button on the page. Sites should strive for an FID of 100 milliseconds or less.

3. Optimize for Mobile On-Page

An essential part of mobile SEO is your On-Page optimization. This includes optimizing key areas of the page for your target keywords, including:

- Meta Title
- Meta Description
- URL
- H1 Tag
- H2-H6 Tags
- Body Content
- Images
- Internal Links
- Navigation Menu

A mobile page that includes your keywords in the right places and the correct number of times can rank higher for those queries.

4. Use Structured Data

Structured data, also known as schema markup, allows Google to better understand the type of content you have on your site. With good structured data in place, your pages can obtain rich results in the search engine results pages (SERPs).

For example, structured data can get your content listed with review stars, recipe images, and event dates in the SERPs, which can significantly increase the click-through rate for your web pages. It can also display your business' name, address, and phone number (NAP) right on the SERPs listing.

5. Optimize for Local Search

According to Google research, "69% of smartphone users turn to mobile search first in a moment of need." And "76% of people who search on their smartphone for something nearby visit a related business within a day." Therefore, a good mobile SEO strategy will include optimizing for local search, as long as your business serves local customers.

Local SEO can help you capture "near me" searches and localized searches with a mobile device. A few good strategies for that include:

- Writing localized content
- Building local backlinks
- Setting up a Google Business Page listing
- Getting customer reviews on Google
- Adding your business NAP information to your website with structured data

6. Specify the Correct Viewport

The viewport is the user's visible area of a web page and it's very important for mobile SEO and responsive design. By specifying the correct viewport, you can ensure that mobile visitors are served the mobile version of your site and not the desktop version.

To optimize your pages correctly, a meta viewport tag must be in the head of the HTML document. This meta viewport tag is what gives the browser instructions on how to control the dimensions and scaling for the page so it is displayed properly for a mobile visitor.

7. Improve Mobile Legibility

If a website is hard to read on a mobile device, then it can cause a poor user experience. Poor user experiences can lead to a drop in rankings as well as if your content does not meet the needs of your users.

Use large fonts and good spacing between paragraph lines so the content is more legible and easier to read on a mobile screen. This also makes it easier on older people and people with disabilities.

8. Improve Tap Target Sizes

According to Google Developers, "interactive elements like buttons or links need to be large enough, and have enough space around them, to make them easy to press without accidentally overlapping onto other elements."

Google Developers go on to say that "A minimum recommended touch target size is around 48 device independent pixels on a site with a properly set mobile viewport.

9. Don't Use Interstitials or Pop-Ups

Google has stated, "Pages that show intrusive interstitials provide a poorer experience to users than other pages where content is immediately accessible." In addition, "Pages where content is not easily accessible to a user on the transition from the mobile search results may not rank as highly."

So you can see it's best not to use interstitials or pop-ups on the mobile version of your site.

10. Monitor, Analyze & Test

As with all SEO practices, optimizing for mobile SEO is not a one-time project.

You need to continue to monitor your results, analyze the data, and test new strategies to find more winning opportunities.

Make sure to set up and regularly check your Google Analytics and Google Search Console for trends in keyword rankings, click-through rates, bounce rates, dwell time, and other metrics for your content.

Below, on the next page or a separate piece of paper, ensure that your content, regardless of whether it's on a website or blog, is optimized for mobile SEO.

CHECKLIST TO ENSURE ALL OF YOUR CONTENT IS OPTIMIZED FOR MOBILE SEO

Content _____

❑ Mobile friendly

❑ Loads fast

❑ Resist the urge to use pop-ups

❑ Use HTML5 instead of Flash

❑ Don't block images, CSS or Javascript

❑ Consider the size of your links/buttons

❑ Use succinct titles, URLs and meta descriptions

❑ Use Schema.org structured data

❑ Optimize for local search

Content _____

❑ Mobile friendly

❑ Loads fast

❑ Resist the urge to use pop-ups

❑ Use HTML5 instead of Flash

❑ Don't block images, CSS or Javascript

❑ Consider the size of your links/buttons

❑ Use succinct titles, URLs and meta descriptions

❑ Use Schema.org structured data

❑ Optimize for local search

Content _____

❑ Mobile friendly

❑ Loads fast

❑ Resist the urge to use pop-ups

❑ Use HTML5 instead of Flash

❑ Don't block images, CSS or Javascript

❑ Consider the size of your links/buttons

❑ Use succinct titles, URLs and meta descriptions

❑ Use Schema.org structured data

❑ Optimize for local search

Content _____

❑ Mobile friendly

❑ Loads fast

❑ Resist the urge to use pop-ups

❑ Use HTML5 instead of Flash

❑ Don't block images, CSS or Javascript

❑ Consider the size of your links/buttons

❑ Use succinct titles, URLs and meta descriptions

❑ Use Schema.org structured data

❑ Optimize for local search

Content _____

❑ Mobile friendly

❑ Loads fast

❑ Resist the urge to use pop-ups

❑ Use HTML5 instead of Flash

❑ Don't block images, CSS or Javascript

❑ Consider the size of your links/buttons

❑ Use succinct titles, URLs and meta descriptions

❑ Use Schema.org structured data

❑ Optimize for local search

CHAPTER 29

THE VISION OF VOICE SEO

Voice search is on the rise. That makes **NOW** a great time for you to learn all about it! Is voice search SEO **really** that important? The latest advancements in technology have made voice searching more accessible than ever.

Nowadays, virtually every modern-day smartphone is equipped with a personal assistant that can be activated via voice. Not only that, but many people also buy smart speakers that can answer your questions, play your favorite music, and much more.

Yes, it is.

Whether it's because of convenience, entertainment, or any other reason, the latest stats show that voice search is a part of a daily routine for millions of people. Think about how often you ask Siri, Alexa, Google, etc. something. It's also one of the biggest reasons why you need to optimize your website for voice search.

Why do we like voice search so much? Well, first of all, it's much faster than turning on a computer and typing. But here are some other reasons we like voice search so much.

- The answers come back quickly with no clicking involved
- You can ask your smartphone something immediately when you think of it
- AI remembers your questions, and you can easily dive into further conversation
- You don't have to worry about spelling errors

With so many people using voice search, you want to be sure your website is optimized for it as well. Here are some ways to optimize your website for voice.

1. Use Long-Tail Keywords

Brands must have actionable keywords and put them in the website's schema markup, also known as code. This will allow the website to provide search engines with more information, which will be important for specific searches people make.

2. Transform Queries into Questions

Instead of using "burger" as a keyword, use something that a voice search user would say, such as "Where can I find a burger near me?" This will make it more likely that your website will be the answer they hear when asking a question.

3. Design for Mobile

There are no design standards for voice search yet, so mobile is the next best thing. Therefore, you want to make sure you have your content designed for mobile. The same metadata is used for voice.

4. Use More Conversational Language

Optimizing for voice search you should make your content conversational.

5. Polish Your 'Google Business Page' Profile

Most voice searches are for local businesses, so think of people who want to know where the nearest gym and restaurant are.

For local businesses, having an updated Google Business Page profile with the name, hours, street address and other relevant information will increase the brand's search ranking and traffic.

6. Localize Your Experience

To optimize for local search, here is what companies should do:

- Include your region in the content and metadata.
- Create location-specific pages with more than just a footer address.
- Use visuals specific to your local area with alt-text tags.
- Tag images and videos with the name of the geographic area.
- If videos and audio discuss a specific location, provide a transcript to boost your website's accessibility.

WHAT IS VOICE SEARCH?

The best way to learn how to take advantage of voice search and use it as a part of your SEO strategy is to understand how it works. Voice search is based on speech recognition technology that converts audio into text. As a result, all we need to do is activate our voice assistants by saying "Hey, Google" or "Hey, Siri" and ask them a question instead of typing it in a search bar.

Modern-day voice command devices go far beyond that and are much more intuitive and capable of recognizing semantics and intent. I find the whole process fascinating. Today you can ask your virtual assistant, "Is it going to rain this weekend?" and it will recognize your intent. It'll understand that you're referring to the upcoming Saturday and Sunday. It will also take into account your location and provide you with a local forecast for the weekend.

This is one example of how voice search works. Since it allows us to browse the web when our hands are busy, some popular voice search trends are asking for directions while driving or looking for recipes while meal prepping. I recently needed directions and of course, I asked Siri. Voice search is also used for shopping, finding information about businesses, products, services, and much more.

In addition, many modern voice-activated devices like smart home speakers are integral parts of smart homes and can be used to control other devices such as controlling your TV, smart lights, smart plugs that can turn a device on or off, etc.

So now that we know the basics of how voice search works, how do I use voice search for SEO? Well, the way you use voice search for SEO depends on your business. Your entire strategy and keyword research should be centered around the product or service your business offers. In addition to that, there are several things you should consider that can make your SEO strategy a lot more successful.

One good thing to remember is that **mobile plays a major role in voice search so you should put a lot of effort into optimizing your website for smartphones if you want to improve your voice search SEO.** Most voice searches occur on mobile, and a high percentage of those mobile voice searches are location-based queries so often users inquire about local businesses, such as restaurants or hotels and will look up the address, opening hours, and similar information. This is why you should make sure to optimize for "near me" searches. Please remember to keep your information updated.

Another aspect of voice search and how it affects SEO efforts is Frequently Asked Questions (FAQs) pages and their structure. Your FAQ pages should feature specific words and phrases. If structured well, the FAQ page will give all the right answers to common questions. Remember to also target long-tail keywords, which we often use when doing a voice search. They also help complete questions and answers. Think about the last time you asked a question? Did it include long-tail keywords? Odds are that it did and you didn't realize it.

WHY VOICE SEARCH SHOULD BE A PART OF MY MARKETING STRATEGY

The possibilities for the future of voice technology are endless, and right now one thing is clear: voice search is taking off among consumers who love the latest electronic home voice assistant devices, including but not limited to including Amazon's Echo and Google Home.

And just as quickly as voice is taking off among consumers, it is also driving a need among businesses to develop a voice search strategy to incorporate into their digital marketing plans, because voice is changing the way people search for and find brands to interact with.

Voice search is a very popular emerging technology that will only keep getting bigger, and as it does it will change the way SEO is done. It can help you improve the customer experience and drive more traffic to your site, and help you stay ahead of the competition.

VOICE TECHNOLOGY IS ON THE RISE AND WILL CONTINUE TO GROW

Voice technology is improving all the time, and as it does consumers are becoming increasingly interested, which means that voice technology isn't going anywhere. Just as smartphones and social media have become permanent fixtures in the digital world, so too will voice technology soon become an integral part of life. It's so incredible the rate that technology advances. There are already 45 million voice-assisted devices in use in the United States alone. Can you believe it?

That means businesses who want to remain visible to consumers in the coming years will have to find a way to incorporate voice technology into their digital marketing strategies.

A VOICE STRATEGY CAN IMPROVE CUSTOMER EXPERIENCE

At the center of any strategy is improving the customer experience. Adopting a voice search strategy isn't just about remaining relevant, it's also about creating a unique and optimized customer experience that will foster relationships and build brand loyalty.

Alexa and Google Assistant can both differentiate between voices, so they can provide valuable insights about users that can lead to more personalized messages and content, and this is great for improving the customer experience. Moreover, voice technology can make interactions with brands more natural and seamless, which encourages retention and loyalty. Come on, you know you enjoy personalized experiences.

Finally, voice search interactions take far less time than text-based ones, which makes life much more convenient for busy consumers who expect a stellar experience and instant gratification every time they interact with a brand.

One example of a brand that has successfully incorporated voice technology into their strategy to set themselves apart from the competition is Whirlpool. They joined with Amazon to create a line of intelligent and voice-activated appliances that can converse with customers, answer questions, and even provide guidance about things like what ingredients a person should buy.

When you knock customer experience out of the park on this level, you're guaranteed to have customers for life.

VOICE TECHNOLOGY IS CHANGING THE FACE OF SEO

Another reason it's important for businesses today to incorporate voice into their digital marketing strategies is because voice search is driving changes in SEO best practices

One of the main reasons for these changes is the fact that people interact with search queries differently when they're posed vocally rather than textually. For example, voice queries tend to be slightly longer than text searches. You can address this by incorporating some longer (at least three words) keyword phrases into your content. Remember your long-tail keywords from earlier in this workbook?

Voice searches also tend to be posed in the form of full questions, such as "will it rain today" instead of just weather, so businesses can also start using relevant question keyword phrases that reflect what prospects might be asking. Another way that voice is going to impact SEO is through the increasing importance of local SEO because many mobile voice searches have a local intent, such as locating a nearby business.

With voice searches, users don't see a full search engine result page and then decide from there which link to click, but rather are presented with the top result or answer. As such, businesses will no longer be vying for a place on page one, but rather for the top result every time, for every search term. What's more, Google Assistant specifically seems to be focusing on featured snippets when providing answers to users, so this means businesses will have to incorporate these best practices into their SEO campaigns as well.

USING VOICE SEARCH TO DRIVE TRAFFIC

While all the possibilities of voice technology haven't yet been fully explored and there are still many questions to be answered, one thing that seems clear is that businesses with voice strategies will be rewarded with higher web traffic.

The way this works is that when a voice assistant provides an answer, it will also provide users with the ability to open the website from which the answer was pulled. For businesses that are successful with voice-optimized SEO, this could mean a great increase in traffic if you often appear as the top result or featured snippet that gets used for voice answers.

CUSTOMERS MAY FIND YOUR COMPETITORS MORE EASILY IF YOU DON'T ADOPT A VOICE SEARCH STRATEGY

Having a voice search strategy today isn't just important for ensuring your customers can find you, but it's also critical when you want to prevent prospects from finding your competition instead.

If your competitors have a voice strategy and you don't, then there's a good chance they'll be found more often thanks to their competitive SEO strategy and ability to adapt to new technologies. Voice technology is still new enough that not a lot of brands have jumped on the bandwagon, and this gives you a great opportunity to get a head start in the game and a leg up on the competition.

THIS IS HOW I WILL INCORPORATE VOICE SEARCH INTO MY MARKETING & SEO STRATEGY

_____

_____

_____

_____

_____

_____

_____

_____

_____

_____

_____

_____

_____

_____

_____

_____

_____

CHAPTER 30
SEO FOR VOICE SEARCH

I'm a big science fiction fan and loved watching the original Star Trek series. While not a fan of Star Trek: The Next Generation, which aired in the mid 1980's, I was fascinated as to how people had conversations with the computer. At the time, having a casual conversation with a computer must have seemed like far-flung science fiction. While that was a television show, I hoped it would become reality as much of science fiction has. Today, we see people speaking into their watches, interacting, and getting voice responses from their phones. The allure of voice chat is undeniable.

Voice search is one of the fastest-growing types of search.

- 55% of users do voice search on a smartphone to ask questions
- 39.4% of U.S. Internet users operate a voice assistant at least once a month, if not more often

Voice search is not a fad and as voice search evolves from voice recognition to voice understanding, Google gets nearer to its aim to transform voice search into "an ultimate mobile assistant that helps you with your daily life so that you can focus on the things that matter." If voice search optimization isn't already part of your SEO strategy, it's time to change that.

Here are 6 Strategies for Voice Search Optimization Success

1. Understand Your Type of Customer & Device Behavior

Just as voice search algorithms use data, location, and several data points to understand search context, marketers have to dig deeper into understanding the consumer and their behavior.

2. Focus on Conversational Keywords

While I don't believe that short tail keywords will ever really disappear, more than ever, marketers need to focus attention on conversational long-tail keywords.

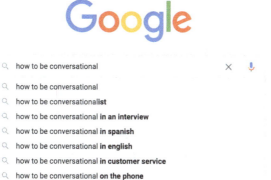

It's essential to work out what questions you need to complete to answer.

3. Create Compelling Persona-Based Content

Brevity, context, and relevance are essential when optimizing for voice search. What might be different from your usual SEO strategy is that now you also need to pay special attention to:

- Creating detailed answers to common questions
- Answering simple questions clearly and concisely.

4. Provide Context with Schema Markup

Get acquainted with schema markup if you aren't already. Use schema to mark up your content and tell search engines what your site's about.

5. Build Pages That Answer FAQs

When voice searchers ask a question, they typically begin it with "Who," "What," "Where," "When," "Why," and "How." They're looking for answers that fulfill an immediate need. To answer these queries, make an FAQ page and begin each question with these adverbs. Then answer them conversationally to appeal to voice search.

6. Think Mobile & Think Local

We have shifted to a Mobile-First world where devices and people are mobile. As a result, it is important to remember that mobile and local go hand in hand, especially where voice search is concerned. Make sure things like directions to brick-and-mortar locations and XML sitemaps are readable to visitors and search engines on your website.

VOICE SEARCH OPTIMIZATION MOVING FORWARD

Voice search is clearly on the rise, and we'd be foolish to ignore this trend in the SEO industry. It's time to stop thinking about it and optimize for voice as it is a winner-take-all search result.

Below or a separate piece of paper, go through your web pages, blogs and content to ensure you are following the strategies for voice search optimization success mentioned in this chapter.

Webpage/Blog/Content _____

❏ Understanding my type of customer & device

❏ Focusing on conversational keywords

❏ Creating compelling persona-based content

❏ Provides context with Schema Markup

❏ My pages answer FAQs

❏ Directions, XML sitemaps are readable to my visitors and search engines

Webpage/Blog/Content _____

❑ Understanding my type of customer & device

❑ Focusing on conversational keywords

❑ Creating compelling persona-based content

❑ Provides context with Schema Markup

❑ My pages answer FAQs

❑ Directions, XML sitemaps are readable to my visitors and search engines

Webpage/Blog/Content _____

❑ Understanding my type of customer & device

❑ Focusing on conversational keywords

❑ Creating compelling persona-based content

❑ Provides context with Schema Markup

❑ My pages answer FAQs

❑ Directions, XML sitemaps are readable to my visitors and search engines

Webpage/Blog/Content _____

❑ Understanding my type of customer & device

❑ Focusing on conversational keywords

❑ Creating compelling persona-based content

❑ Provides context with Schema Markup

❑ My pages answer FAQs

❑ Directions, XML sitemaps are readable to my visitors and search engines

Webpage/Blog/Content _____

❑ Understanding my type of customer & device

❑ Focusing on conversational keywords

❑ Creating compelling persona-based content

❑ Provides context with Schema Markup

❑ My pages answer FAQs

❑ Directions, XML sitemaps are readable to my visitors and search engines

CHAPTER 31
THE NOT SO ULTIMATE GUIDE TO E-COMMERCE SEO

Getting more traffic is top of mind for any E-commerce business owner, so the thought of mastering E-commerce SEO has probably crossed your mind once or twice. Consistent, high-quality organic traffic you **DON'T** have to pay for? That works for me!

E-commerce SEO is the search engine optimization of an online store. Writing long descriptions with relevant keywords on every product page is an example of E-commerce optimization. Obtaining backlinks from relevant websites can also improve your online store's ranking position.

E-commerce SEO is the process of generating more organic traffic from sites like Google, Bing, and Yahoo to your online store. When you search for women's t-shirts on Google, for example, you're taken to the search engine results page (SERP) shown below.

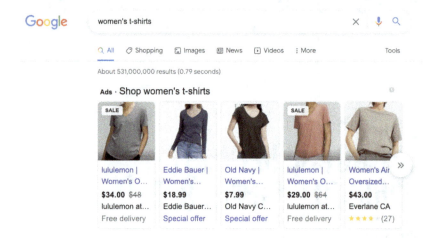

Of course, as with all organic SEO the further you get from page 1 of the SERPS, the less traffic you will see. The goal is to rank as high on the first page of search engines like Google, Bing, and Yahoo as you can for search terms that your potential customers might be using.

E-commerce is a huge industry so optimizing an E-commerce website is more complex than working on a blog or corporate website. You have many more pages to optimize, and it's much more difficult to promote an E-commerce website.

The most important E-commerce SEO factors are:

- Optimization of an online shop starts with the homepage and category pages. These two-page types have to be properly optimized before you start working on your product pages.
- Optimize your product pages based on the results of your keyword research.
- Optimize **ALL** visual elements of your store (images, videos)
- Add the necessary schemas (product, offers, etc.)
- Promote your store on social media networks.
- Think of creative ways to get people to link to your product pages.

- Start a blog and publish content related to your products and how they can help people solve a problem.

Search Engine Optimization (SEO) is a long-term, challenging battle that requires consistent improvement for your E-commerce website by following a customized strategy to reach the first position for desired search results. The reason E-commerce SEO is tougher is because companies battle each other as there are hundreds or maybe thousands of stores competing for the same keywords related to products or product categories.

So why invest in E-commerce SEO? E-commerce SEO is very important because more than 45% of online shopping transactions start on search engines where a potential customer performs a search with transaction search queries like using the name of desired products and in more than 90% of cases, they will visit only the first 3 results of websites and online stores on the first search engine results page.

The main steps for an efficient E-commerce SEO strategy are:

1. E-commerce Keyword Research

E-commerce keyword research is more technical and critical than keyword research for other types of websites as your main aim is to choose keywords suitable for transactional search queries that are performed by potential customers in order to find suitable products to satisfy their needs and eventually buying them from the E-commerce store that appears in the first search results and provides exceptional online shopping experiences.

2. Improving the E-commerce Website Structure

The user experience is a critical ranking factor for search engines as they aim to guarantee the best navigation experience for search engine users by displaying only the websites that care about that aspect and decrease the bounce rate of online store visits.

3. On-Page SEO for Product & Category Pages

On-Page SEO is a key factor for your E-commerce store to reach higher ranking in targeted search results, increase the clicks on your website search results, driving more conversions and sales and the overall success of your E-commerce SEO plan.

4. Handling E-commerce Technical SEO Issues

E-commerce websites are known for the many increasing pages for products and categories and with more pages available, there will be more Technical SEO aspects & issues to care about.

An efficient E-commerce SEO process requires performing periodic site audits "weekly or twice a month" to uncover and to handle Technical SEO issues to avoid losing achieved higher ranking on search results or providing poor user experience

5. E-commerce Link-Building

E-commerce link-building is a tough challenge as not many websites or blogs are willing to refer to a website that consists of products rather than valuable related content.

Despite how challenging it is, link-building is essential for your E-commerce SEO strategy. It increases and demonstrates your E-commerce website authority to search engines to improve ranking in targeted search results and to earn referral traffic.

An effective E-commerce link-building strategy will require performing detailed analyses of your backlinks profile and also the competitors' backlinks profiles to define worthy link-building opportunities and your outreach plan.

Below, on the next page or on a separate piece of paper, create an E-commerce SEO strategy for your online store. If you don't have a store, create a fictional one.

THIS IS MY E-COMMERCE SEO STRATEGY FOR MY STORE

_____

_____

_____

_____

_____

_____

_____

_____

_____

_____

_____

_____

_____

_____

_____

_____

_____

_____

_____

_____

_____

_____

_____

_____

_____

_____

_____

_____

_____

_____

_____

_____

_____

_____

_____

CHAPTER 32
USING WHITE HAT SEO INSTEAD OF BLACK HAT SEO MAKES A DIFFERENCE

Some people consider 'Black Hat SEO' as being a type of SEO, and this creates confusion for beginners. Black Hat SEO is just a term that is used to describe any actions taken to trick search engine algorithms. From time to time, people come up with ideas on how to artificially create links to improve the rankings of a website on Google. These methods go against Google guidelines and should be avoided.

Black Hat SEO

Tactics that are used to rank a website that violates search engine guidleines. Black Hat SEO techniques attempt to manipulate search engine algorithms to increase a site's rankings on the SERPs.

White Hat SEO

A set of SEO strategies that improve your site's rankings on a search engine results page without violating the rules of the search engine.

- Duplicate Content
- Keyword Stuffing
- Link Farming
- Cloaking Text and/or Links

- Fresh, Relevant Content
- Linking to/Getting Links from Relevant Industry Sources
- Relevant Page Titles & Tags
- Natural Keyword Density

The only outcome from following Black Hat techniques is to lose your Google rankings and trust, get penalized by Google, and diminish your chances of achieving any rankings in Google ever again.

On the other hand, "White Hat SEO" refers to SEO tactics that are in line with the terms and conditions of the major search engines, including Google. White Hat SEO is the opposite of Black Hat SEO.

Examples of White Hat SEO include:

- Offering quality content and services
- Fast site loading times and mobile-friendliness
- Using descriptive, keyword-rich meta tags
- Making your site easy to navigate

On the next page or a separate piece of paper, research and list all the White Hat SEO techniques and ensure you use the White Hat techniques and not the Black Hat with your content.

WHITE HAT TECHNIQUES

BLACK HAT TECHNIQUES

_____   _____
_____   _____
_____   _____
_____   _____
_____   _____
_____   _____
_____   _____
_____   _____
_____   _____
_____   _____
_____   _____
_____   _____
_____   _____
_____   _____
_____   _____
_____   _____
_____   _____
_____   _____
_____   _____
_____   _____
_____   _____
_____   _____
_____   _____
_____   _____
_____   _____
_____   _____
_____   _____
_____   _____
_____   _____
_____   _____

CHAPTER 33
WHY FOLLOWING CORE WEB VITALS IS CRITICAL TO YOUR SUCCESS

In June 2021, Google updated its algorithms to incorporate a new ranking factor: Page Experience. To measure Page Experience, Google developed a new set of metrics called the Web Vitals. You can find three core metrics within these Web Vitals: Largest Contentful Paint, First Input Delay, and Cumulative Layout Shift. These stand for performance, responsiveness, and visual stability, the three pillars of Google's Page Experience update.

Core Web Vitals becoming ranking signals is an important shift in how search engine rankings work. Now, the user experience will play a tangible role if your website reaches that coveted number one spot. A poorly designed website with no focus on user experience just won't cut it.

By including Core Web Vitals as search engine ranking factors, Google aims to help website owners build pages with user experience in mind – not just cranking out content related to their topic with no thought for whether or not it's an overall enjoyable experience for the user.

This doesn't mean that you should disregard the content of your site by any means. As Google itself states:

"A good Page Experience doesn't override having great, relevant content. However, in cases where multiple pages have similar content, Page Experience becomes much more important for visibility in search."

Optimizing Page Experience should be done hand in hand with crafting quality, relevant content. These two together can give you the upper hand over your competitors.

For example, if there are two pages, both providing something similar in terms of content and quality, the page with the better user experience (as measured by Google's Core Web Vitals) will win the battle and rank higher in search results.

WHAT ARE CORE WEB VITALS AND WHY ARE THEY IMPORTANT?

Core Web Vitals are a set of specific factors that Google considers important in a webpage's overall user experience. Core Web Vitals consist of three specific page speed and user interaction measurements: largest contentful paint, first input delay, and cumulative layout shift.

In short, Core Web Vitals are a subset of factors that will be part of Google's "Page Experience" score (basically, Google's way of sizing up your page's overall UX, which stands for user experience).

Core Web Vitals Are Part Of Google's Overall Evaluation Of "Page Experience"

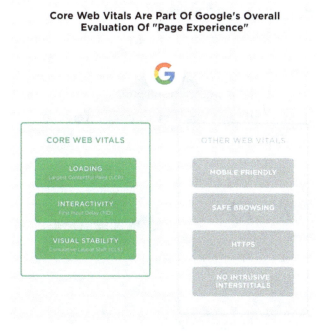

Google plans to make Page Experience an official Google ranking factor and Core Web Vitals will be a super important part of that score.

It's important for us to point out that a great Page Experience score won't magically push you to the #1 spot in Google. In fact, Google was quick to point out that Page Experience is one of 200+ ranking factors that they use.

Core Web Vitals are a subset of Web Vitals that apply to all web pages and should be measured by all site owners. They will be across all Google tools. Each of the Core Web Vitals represents a distinct facet of the user experience, is measurable in the field, and reflects the real-world experience of a critical user-centric outcome.

LARGEST CONTENTFUL PAINT (LCP)

LCP is how long it takes a page to load from the point of view of an actual user. In other words, it's the time from clicking on a link to seeing the majority of the content on-screen.

These elements might include images, videos, or other types of content. Now that you know what LCP is, you can start optimizing for it. According to Google, you should aim for the LCP to happen within the first 2.5 seconds of the page loading. Everything over 4 seconds needs improvement, and you can consider everything over that as performing poorly.

AN OVERVIEW OF THE SCORING FOR LCP

According to Google, the LCP is affected by several factors:

- Slow server response times: optimize your server, use of a CDN, cache assets, etc.
- Render-blocking JavaScript and CSS: so minify your CSS, defer non-critical CSS, and inline critical CSS.
- Slow-loading resources: so optimize your images, preload resources, compress text files, etc.
- Issues on client-side rendering: so minimize critical JavaScript, and use server-side rendering and pre-rendering.

FID: FIRST INPUT DELAY

The First Input Delay measures the time it takes for the browser to respond to the user's first interaction. The faster the browser reacts, the more responsive the page will appear. If you are looking to offer your users a positive experience, and that should be your main goal, then you should work on your pages' responsiveness.

Delays happen when the browser is still doing other work in the background. So it has loaded the page, and everything looks great, but when you tap that button, nothing happens! That's a bad experience, and it leads to frustration. Even if there's just a small delay, it might make your site feel sluggish and unresponsive.

The FID measures all interactions that happen during the loading of the page. These are input actions like taps, clicks, and key presses, but not interactions like zooming and scrolling. Google's new metrics call for an FID of less than 100ms to appear responsive. Anything between 100ms and 300ms needs improvement, and you can view anything above that as performing poorly.

After testing the FID you get a score, and you can work from there. There are always improvements to make, but you have to decide if that's worth it.

CLS: CUMULATIVE LAYOUT SHIFT

The third Core Web Vital is a brand-new one called Cumulative Layout Shift. This metric determines how 'stable' stuff loads onto your screen.

These layout shifts happen a lot with ads. Ads are a lifeline for many sites, but these are often loaded so poorly that they frustrate users. Also, many complex sites have so much going on that these are heavy to load, and content gets loaded whenever it's ready. This can also result in content or CTAs that jump around on the screen, making room for slower loading content. For example, news websites are typically very complex and slow to load.

The Cumulative Layout Shift compares frames to determine the movement of elements. It takes all the points at which layout shifts happen and calculates the severity of those movements. As you can see from the image below, Google considers anything below 0.1 good, while anything from 0.1 to 0.25 needs work. You can consider everything above 0.25 as poor.

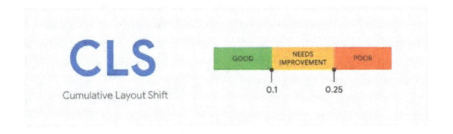

THE SCORES FOR CLS

Take some time and look at your website to see if it meets the Core Web Vitals. Vitals is time well invested, and as you can see, Core Web Vitals is not going anywhere.

Use the next page or a separate sheet of paper to write down your Core Web Vitals, see where they should be, and ways you can improve them.

THIS IS MY STRATEGY TO IMPROVE MY CORE WEB VITALS

_____

_____

_____

_____

_____

_____

_____

_____

_____

_____

_____

_____

_____

_____

_____

_____

_____

_____

_____

_____

_____

_____

CHAPTER 34
WHAT IS YMYL?

YMYL stands for "Your Money or Your Life." Google uses this acronym as a guiding principle for classifying pages that impact your finances, health, safety, and/or happiness.

YMYL sites are held to the highest possible E-A-T standards due to the subject matter and what it means for a user if that information is misrepresented.

According to Google:

> "We have very high Page Quality rating standards for YMYL pages because low-quality YMYL pages could negatively impact a person's happiness, health, financial stability, or safety."

TYPES OF YMYL WEBSITES

The pages most often considered YMYL include:

- **News and Current Events**: Topics that cover areas such as international events, business, politics, science, and technology (Not all news falls under YMYL, such as entertainment and sports, though you should strive for high E-A-T regardless to improve your content's profile.)
- **Civics, Government, Law**: The dissemination of information that pertains to voting, government agencies, public institutions, social services, or legal advice
- **Finance**: Any financial advice or information regarding investments, taxes, retirement planning, loans, banking, or insurance
- **Shopping**: E-commerce content that features product research or the researching of goods and services that involve a purchase
- **Health and Safety**: Content that features or dispenses information or advice on health and medical issues, including hospitals and pharmacies, or drugs (emergency preparedness or content that defines or discusses dangerous activities)
- **Groups of People**: Content that features information or claims about people based on ethnicity, race, or nationality, religion, age or disability, gender (gender identity), sexual orientation, or veteran status

The list may also include more subjective topics and content based on their context or how the information is presented. Such items might consist of parenting information, information on housing or remodeling, researching schools or colleges, finding employment, or matters on fitness, nutrition, or weight loss

If your site is covered under YMYL, go through each page to ensure your content follows the highest possible guidelines. If any of the content isn't, use the space on the next few pages to re-write it.

WEBSITE NAME: _____

Web Page: _____

EXPERTISE

WHAT NEEDS TO BE FIXED

_____

_____

_____

_____

_____

_____

_____

_____

_____

_____

_____

_____

_____

_____

WEBSITE NAME: _____

Web Page: _____

AUTHORITY

WHAT NEEDS TO BE FIXED

_____

_____

_____

_____

_____

_____

_____

_____

_____

_____

_____

_____

_____

_____

WEBSITE NAME: _____

Web Page: _____

TRUST

WHAT NEEDS TO BE FIXED

_____

_____

_____

_____

_____

_____

_____

_____

_____

_____

_____

_____

_____

_____

_____

WEBSITE NAME: _____

Web Page: _____

EXPERTISE

       ❑ Page 1   ❑ Page 2   ❑ Page 3

       ❑ Page 4   ❑ Page 5   ❑ Page 6

       ❑ Page 7   ❑ Page 8   ❑ Page 9

       ❑ Page 10   ❑ Page 11   ❑ Page 12

       ❑ Page 13   ❑ Page 14   ❑ Page 15

       ❑ Page 16   ❑ Page 17   ❑ Page 18

       ❑ Page 19   ❑ Page 20   ❑ Page 21

       ❑ Page 22   ❑ Page 23   ❑ Page 24

WHAT NEEDS TO BE FIXED

_____

_____

_____

_____

_____

_____

_____

_____

_____

_____

_____

_____

_____

_____

_____

_____

_____

_____

WEBSITE NAME: _____

Web Page: _____

AUTHORITY

❑ Page 1	❑ Page 2	❑ Page 3
❑ Page 4	❑ Page 5	❑ Page 6
❑ Page 7	❑ Page 8	❑ Page 9
❑ Page 10	❑ Page 11	❑ Page 12
❑ Page 13	❑ Page 14	❑ Page 15
❑ Page 16	❑ Page 17	❑ Page 18
❑ Page 19	❑ Page 20	❑ Page 21
❑ Page 22	❑ Page 23	❑ Page 24

WHAT NEEDS TO BE FIXED

_____
_____
_____
_____
_____
_____
_____
_____
_____
_____
_____
_____
_____
_____
_____
_____
_____
_____

WEBSITE NAME: _____

Web Page: _____

TRUST

    ❏ Page 1   ❏ Page 2   ❏ Page 3

    ❏ Page 4   ❏ Page 5   ❏ Page 6

    ❏ Page 7   ❏ Page 8   ❏ Page 9

    ❏ Page 10   ❏ Page 11   ❏ Page 12

    ❏ Page 13   ❏ Page 14   ❏ Page 15

    ❏ Page 16   ❏ Page 17   ❏ Page 18

    ❏ Page 19   ❏ Page 20   ❏ Page 21

    ❏ Page 22   ❏ Page 23   ❏ Page 24

WHAT NEEDS TO BE FIXED

_____
_____
_____
_____
_____
_____
_____
_____
_____
_____
_____
_____
_____
_____
_____
_____
_____
_____
_____

CHAPTER 35
EAT YOUR WAY TO SUCCESS WITH E-A-T

E-A-T stands for Expertise, Authoritativeness, and Trustworthiness. It comes from Google's Search Quality Rater Guidelines. It is a 168-page document used by human quality raters to assess the quality of Google's search results.

E-A-T is important for all queries, but some more so than others. Google refers to these topics as YMYL (Your Money or Your Life) topics. The reason for this is these topics could potentially impact a person's future happiness, health, financial stability, or safety. If your site is built around a YMYL topic, then demonstrating EAT is crucial.

HOW DOES GOOGLE DETERMINE E-A-T?

So now that you know what E-A-T is, let's talk about how Google determines the E-A-T of a page. At a high level, there are three primary components listed in the Google search quality evaluator guidelines:

- The Expertise of the creator of the main content.
- The Authoritativeness of the creator of the main content, the main content itself, and the website.
- The Trustworthiness of the creator of the main content, the main content itself, and the website.

ENSURING ACCURATE, TRUTHFUL, USEFUL INFORMATION

Essentially, E-A-T is one way Google tries to ensure that it returns accurate, truthful, useful information to searchers. Anyone can create a website and publish whatever they want on it. You don't have to be a doctor to start a medical information website or have a finance degree to write about investing.

Of course, this is a double edge sword as it also presents a problem for Google. People make important decisions based on what they learn from search results, so Google aims to ensure that those decisions are based on the most trustworthy information possible. As a result, Google considers the Expertise, Authoritativeness, and Trustworthiness of the individual creator of page content, the content itself, and the entire website. In Google's eyes, a thorough medical article written by an experienced doctor at the Mayo Clinic website is much more valuable than a random blog post dispensing unverified medical advice.

EXPERTISE: DOES YOUR CONTENT DEMONSTRATE YOUR EXPERTISE?

Expertise means having a high level of knowledge or skill in a particular field. It's evaluated primarily at the content level, not at the website or organizational level. Google is looking for content created by a subject matter expert.

For YMYL topics, this is about the formal expertise, qualifications, and education of the content creator. An example of this is, that a CPA is more qualified to write about tax preparation than someone who's read a few posts online. Formal expertise is important for YMYL topics such as medical, financial, or legal advice. For non-YMYL topics, it's about demonstrating relevant life experience and "everyday expertise."

Some topics require less formal expertise. For example, Google says that "everyday expertise" is enough for some YMYL topics. For example, take a query like "what does it feel like to have cancer." Someone living with the disease is better placed to answer this than a qualified doctor with years of experience. Sharing personal experience is a form of everyday expertise.

AUTHORITATIVENESS: WHAT DO EXPERTS IN THE FIELD SAY ABOUT YOU?

Authority is about reputation, particularly among other experts and influencers in the industry. When others see an individual or website as the go-to source of information about a topic, that's authority. To evaluate authority, raters search the web for insights into the website's reputation or individuals' reputation.

You can use reputation research to find out what real users, as well as experts, think about a website. Look for reviews, references, recommendations by experts, news articles, and other credible information created/written by individuals about the website. Raters are told to look for independent sources when doing this. It's also the case that some people and websites are uniquely authoritative regarding certain topics. For example, the most authoritative source of lyrics to Coldplay songs is their official website. And the most authoritative source of information for beef grades in the US is the USDA.

TRUSTWORTHINESS: ARE YOU A TRUSTED SOURCE OF INFORMATION IN YOUR FIELD?

Trust is about the legitimacy, transparency, and accuracy of the website and its content. Raters look for several things to evaluate trustworthiness, including whether the website states who is responsible for published content. This is particularly important for YMYL queries but applies to non-YMYL queries too.

YMYL websites demand a high degree of trust, so they generally need satisfying information about who is responsible for the site's content. If a store or financial transaction website has just an email address and physical address, it may be difficult to get help if there are issues with the transaction. Likewise, many other types of YMYL websites also require a high degree of user trust.

Raters also consider content accuracy. For example, news articles and information pages must be factually accurate for the topic and must be supported by expert consensus where such consensus exists. Citing trustworthy sources is part of this. An article with a satisfying amount of accurate information and trustworthy external references can usually be rated in the high range.

Keep in mind that trust, like authoritativeness, is a relative concept. People and websites can't be perceived as trustworthy in all areas. For example, we're a trustworthy source of information about SEO, but not bodybuilding.

As this workbook was being edited, Google added another E to E-A-T for experience, so it is now E-E-A-T.

Google has made significant changes to its Quality Rater Guidelines (QRG) for search. Google updates this document several times per year, and the latest version came with some notable changes to the structure of the document, with many new sections and tables added and a total of 11 new pages worth of content. While there are dozens of important details about what changes, the most important change was the introduction of the letter E to the start of the acronym E-A-T.

INTRODUCING E-E-A-T

Google is now introducing the concept of E-E-A-T, which stands for:

- Experience
- Expertise
- Authoritativeness
- Trustworthiness

The addition of "experience" indicates that content quality can also be evaluated by understanding the extent to which the content creator has first-hand experience in the topic.

With this reframing of E-E-A-T, Google also states that "trust" is at the center of this concept and is the "most important member of the E-E-A-T family."

Google also provides many more clear examples of important concepts, such as:

- Evaluating the reputation of websites and content contributors.
- The extent to which E-E-A-T matters and how it should be evaluated.
- What it means for content to be harmful.

Google appears to be evolving its language to be more inclusive and keep up with the times. It added many new mentions of social media platforms, influencers, and how content can take different forms, such as video, UGC, and social media posts. In this version, Google also takes a granular approach in answering many common questions about how E-E-A-T works and how much it matters for different topics. Google spells out what content should be considered harmful and whether everyday experience is sufficient to produce trustworthy content for the topic at hand. There are many more changes than what is outlined in this workbook.

Below, on the next page, or a separate piece of paper, write out your E-E-A-T regarding your web page or blog. Does your topic fall under YMYL? If so, make certain your topic follows E-E-A-T carefully.

_____

_____

_____

_____

_____

_____

_____

_____

CHAPTER 36
GOING BEYOND THE BORDERS WITH INTERNATIONAL SEO

If your business is doing well in your country, it may be time for you to start thinking about international SEO or even multilingual SEO. If you want to ensure your website will be found and used well in other countries, this requires some extra investments.

International SEO deals with offering optimized content for multiple languages or multiple locations. For example, imagine you have an online store, and you sell WordPress plugins in many countries. Let's say to increase your sales in Germany, you've decided to translate your content into German and create a German site. Now, you have two variations of the same page: English and German versions. Pretty straightforward, huh? Unfortunately no.

Obviously, you want people who search in Germany to be directed to the German site. You may even want to have a specific site for German speakers in Switzerland. It might be even better to have a French alternative for speakers of French in Switzerland as well.

Let's assume for now that you don't have the required resources for that situation. In that case, it's probably best to send users from Switzerland who speak French to the English site. On top of that, you must ensure that you send all other users to your English site, as they are more likely to speak English than German. In a scenario like this, you must set up and implement a multilingual, international SEO strategy. Are you still with me?

WHY INTERNATIONAL SEO IS IMPORTANT

You want your website to be found on Google. In a standard SEO strategy, you optimize your content for one language, the language your website is written in. Sometimes, however, you want to target audiences in multiple countries and regions. Just like in standard SEO, no matter how similar these audiences are, there will always be differences. In this case, one of these differences is substantial. The language they speak. When you make your site available in several languages and target specific regions, you achieve two things:

- You expand your potential audience.
- You improve your chances of ranking for a specific region and in several languages.

It all sounds rather clear-cut, but multilingual SEO can be hard. A lot can go wrong, and a bad multilingual implementation can hurt your rankings. This means that you need to know what you're doing. Here is an example from Apple.

For example, if we Google "apple official website" in the US, this is the first result:

Apple
https://www.apple.com/ ▾
Discover the innovative world of **Apple** and shop everything iPhone, iPad, **Apple** Watch, Mac, and **Apple** TV, plus explore accessories, entertainment, and expert ...

If we do the same in Spain, we see this version of the page:

Apple (España)
https://www.apple.com/es/ ▾ Traduzir esta página
Descubre las novedades de **Apple**, compra el iPhone, iPad, **Apple** Watch, Mac y **Apple** TV, encuentra accesorios y entretenimiento. Y habla con expertos.
iPhone · Mac · iPad · Watch

Hreflang makes this possible.

One of the biggest risks of multilingual SEO is duplicate content. If you present very similar content on your website on multiple pages, again, just as in a standard SEO strategy, Google won't know which content to show in the search engines. Duplicate pages compete with each other, so the individual rankings of the pages will go down.

TECHNICAL INTERNATIONAL SEO

1. Site Structure: Language, Country, or Hybrid

It may seem obvious, but before you do any optimization or site structuring, you need to figure out which languages or regions you want to target. Language targeting may be the easiest route to go because there are fewer languages than countries in the world.

The one thing you need to pay attention to is the difference between language and country. For example, if you target Spanish, your website may yield an enormous global audience, but remember readers from Spain and Puerto Rico will have different needs and expectations.

Hreflang is an HTML attribute used to specify the language and geographical targeting of a webpage. If you have multiple versions of the same page in different languages, you can use the hreflang tag to tell search engines like Google about these variations. This helps them to provide the correct version to their users.

> Subfolders: example.com/en/
>
> - This option is preferable because it's easier to modify in the future
>
> Subdomains: en.example.com
>
> Parameters: example.com/?lang=en

Country-level targeting can be useful for companies whose content changes depending on location, such as retailers that offer distinct products, shipping, customer service, pricing, or images based on a user's country. Country-level targeting can also help you abide by local regulations. If you choose country-level targeting, here is how you can structure your site.

> Here is how you can structure your site if you go down the country route:
>
> Subfolders: example.com/us/
>
> Country code top-level domains (ccTLDs): example.us
>
> Subdomains: us.example.com
>
> Separate domains: anotherexample.com
>
> *Note: It is NOT recommended to use separate domains since it will dilute the authority you've earned from your main domain.

On the next page or a separate page, play with the different options talked about in this section. Please note, before making **ANY** changes, I recommend that you make a copy of whatever file you are working on so you have the original intact if something goes wrong.

2. Implementing Hreflang To Avoid Cannibalization

As mentioned previously, your site may have multiple versions of a page that target different languages or countries. If search engines see those pages as identical, you could experience a loss in rankings due to rank cannibalization.

Let's say you have a product page that ranks well on Google in the United States. You plan to launch in Australia and Switzerland, so you create new versions of that page for each region. Sounds good, right? Well, to avoid cannibalization, you want to tag the entire "cluster" of pages with all of the languages and countries you are targeting. Therefore, your hreflang tags or attributes would look like this:

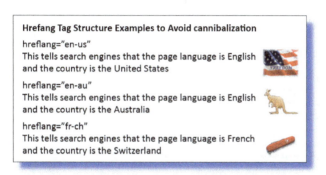

Hrefang Tag Structure Examples to Avoid cannibalization

hreflang="en-us"
This tells search engines that the page language is English and the country is the United States

hreflang="en-au"
This tells search engines that the page language is English and the country is the Australia

hreflang="fr-ch"
This tells search engines that the page language is French and the country is the Switzerland

When correctly implemented, hreflang tags tell search engines to recognize different page versions as "alternates," meaning they will be swapped out depending on where the searcher is located.

Proper implementation of hreflang is challenging, but it improves user experience considerably. That is the most important factor, as visitors to your site will now only see relevant content and currencies. You can be sure that any country-specific-rules and regulations are followed, and your hard-earned ranks will not be affected by cannibalization.

INTERNATIONAL CONTENT SEO

Similar to a standard SEO strategy, once you have a solid technical foundation for your international site(s), the next step is to create content that provides value to users in each region that you care about. Sound familiar?

• • •

Translation vs. Transcreation

Content localization is an art, and simple translation won't cut it. Translation refers to the word-for-word transcription of content from one language to another, however, translation falls short of capturing the full nuance of a piece of content. Not to mention the negative impact it can have on user experience and rankings.

Transcreation, on the other hand, means taking a local cultural context into account. Intent, style, tone, and context can change depending on your audience. For example, consider variations in holidays. In the United States, Black Friday and Cyber Monday are key shopping days. In China, however, Singles' Day is the celebration of consumerism. A business with a presence in both regions must adjust not only sales assets but also content strategies to account for this cultural difference.

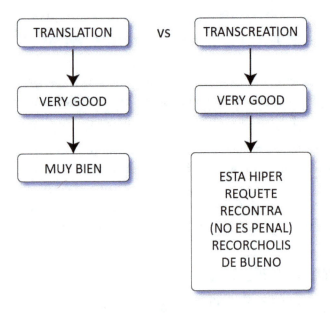

Now, transcreation doesn't simply stop with understanding different holidays. Your target persona can change from country to country.

People that purchase your products in one region may have different demographics from another region.

Besides creating the right content, you also need to set up proper reporting so that you can measure the impact of any changes and share your success. As with everything else with international SEO, KPIs get more complex. You'll want to ensure that your reporting is clear, reproducible and, if possible, consistent across regions. That does not mean that you will always measure the same things. Remember, KPIs in one region may look very different from those in another.

As you can see, there is a lot involved in international SEO, but if your business is ready for it, be prepared and do your research.

WHAT FUNCTIONALITY DO YOU NEED IN AN INTERNATIONAL ENTERPRISE SEO PLATFORM?

Obviously, a global or international SEO strategy has many moving parts. Hence, managing the complexity requires an SEO platform that operates across search engines, audits your technical foundation, and oversees your business' content creation and reporting. So what should you look for?

- Set up your account for success, so track down your most important keywords on the right domains and in the right locations. Make sure your keywords are bucketed into semantically related categories so that it's easier to find insights from the data.

- Research the right search engines to understand your true online presence across the globe. Most enterprise SEO platforms allow you to track data on Google. However, that doesn't account for the 14% of global searchers that use a search engine other than Google.

- Create and manage content for international audiences. Any top SEO platform should not only proactively recommend content for each of your audiences but should also allow you to make changes directly to pages from within the platform itself.

This way, you are bypassing your CMS, and that's important because it lets you conserve valuable developer resources and, as important, make changes fast, thereby responding to real-time performance signals.

Below, on the next page or on a separate piece of paper identify ONE language or region you might want to market to. After that make a list of international enterprise SEO platforms. Then determine and list the functionality you will need on that platform. As a last recommendation, follow through on the bullets above.

_____

_____

_____

_____

_____

_____

_____

_____

ABOUT THE AUTHOR

Carolyn B. Josephs is a Yoast Certified SEO Copywriter & Keyword Researcher, a Certified Constant Contact Solutions Provider, a Hubspot Certified Content Marketer, Udemy Certified Social Media Manager & Creator of Facebook & Instagram Ads as well as LinkedIn Certified in SEO.

Carolyn is a professional designer with extensive experience in print and digital marketing services who is passionate about helping small businesses and non-profit organizations, especially those focused on animal welfare and supporting veterans. Carolyn has decades of experience in traditional graphic design and as the industry evolved so did her skills. During the course of her career, she worked in several industries that all shared a common theme, that of helping others achieve their goals.

facebook.com/CJDesignandConsulting

twitter.com/cbjdesigns

instagram.com/cjdesignandconsulting

linkedin.com/company/cj-design-&-consulting

pinterest.com/cbj1964

youtube.com/@cjdesignconsulting3192

www.ingramcontent.com/pod-product-compliance
Lightning Source LLC
LaVergne TN
LVHW051638050326
832903LV00022B/803